Praise f-

"A combination of *On Golden Pond* and *It's a Wonderful Life*, this inspirational and entertaining book will inspire you to embrace your flaws and strive for a deeper and more meaningful life. As Margaret Terry shares the defining moments of her life in letters to a dying friend, she uncovers vital lessons of strength, love, forgiveness, gratitude, and faith. You will laugh and you will cry, but mostly you will be roused to reach out to those you love, to share secret pieces of your own heart."

—DARLENE GUDRIE BUTTS, AUTHOR,
LESSONS FROM THE DEPRESSION

"To anyone heaped in sorrow, the kindest generosity is not a meal or a gift. It's presence. *Dear Deb* is a beautiful testament to what can happen when one woman chooses to step into another's story through faithfully sharing her own. As one who heard the word *cancer* and survived, I affirm it was the Margaret Terrys in my life who gave me enough courage to keep living."

—MICHELE CUSHATT, INSPIRATIONAL SPEAKER,
DYNAMICS COMMUNICATORS INTERNATIONAL

"Margaret Terry's *Dear Deb* is that steady hand at your elbow at the moment you feel like running away. It's the voice of friendship that says, 'Let's be honest.' Faced with losing her friend by inches to cancer, Terry went looking for miracles, and found them embedded in her own imperfect life. By pouring her secrets out on the page, Terry lights the path toward self-honesty—and self-acceptance—one small candle at a time. The book is a contemplation of gratitude, a vessel of confession, and the surprise of being made whole even after irreversible loss. If you think, *There has to be more to life*, then pick up this book, and follow the fifty-five small candles of honesty to the place Terry leads you. That place, astonishingly, is you."

—BONNIE GROVE, AWARD-WINNING, INTERNATIONALLY
PUBLISHED AUTHOR OF *YOUR BEST YOU: DISCOVERING
AND DEVELOPING THE STRENGTHS GOD GAVE YOU*

"Over 400 years ago, Pascal wrote, 'The heart has reasons of which reason will never understand.' As Margaret Terry courageously shared the stories of her life, she helped a friend face her death. The mysteries of each—life and death—are matters of the heart. *Dear Deb* will do yours good."

—GUY CHEVREAU, AUTHOR OF *WE DANCE BECAUSE WE CANNOT FLY*, *TURNINGS*, AND *CATCH THE FIRE*

"*Dear Deb* is full of heart, love, and inspiring stories. Margaret Terry is a natural storyteller."

—JENNIFER HAUPT, AUTHOR, *I'LL STAND BY YOU: ONE WOMAN'S MISSION TO HEAL THE CHILDREN OF THE WORLD*

"In this honest and tender love letter about life, Margaret Terry shows us how real courage and faith are manifested. When I closed this book, I had one word to say: 'Amen!'"

—ANN HITE, AWARD-WINNING AUTHOR OF *GHOST ON BLACK MOUNTAIN*

"These letters to a dying woman demonstrate the power of stories to make us feel alive and hopeful—even at our lowest moments. Margaret Terry's faith creates a graceful frame for fifty-five small, shining portraits of love, loss, and forgiveness. (For fans of Anne LaMott, here's a kindred spirit!)"

—MARNI JACKSON, AUTHOR, *THE MOTHER ZONE*

"Moving stories of one woman's life that renewed her faith in friendship and in God. . . . The overall effect of these letters is that of faith, hope, and perseverence in the face of adversity."

—*KIRKUS REVIEWS*

"A book in a million. *Dear Deb* takes us over thresholds of truth and transparency rarely crossed."

—LEONARD SWEET, AUTHOR, PROFESSOR (DREW UNIVERSITY, GEORGE FOX UNIVERSITY), AND SEMIOTICIAN

"Margaret Terry's compelling and heart-revealing stories transfuse grace, strength, and encouragement to someone facing life's biggest challenge. Reading the letters in *Dear Deb* is like having a cup of tea with a close friend, sharing a conversation about our deepest joys and sorrows, discovering meaning in our common experience, and coming away feeling love, hope, and affirmation."

—WENDY ELAINE NELLES, AWARD-WINNING WRITER,
EDITOR OF BEST-SELLING *HOT APPLE CIDER* AND *A
SECOND CUP OF HOT APPLE CIDER* INSPIRATIONAL
ANTHOLOGIES, AND CO-FOUNDER OF THE WORD GUILD

"Good friends give each other the most precious pieces of themselves for safekeeping. This book contains the pieces Margaret Terry gave Deb when they both needed a miracle: pieces of hope and heart, faith and courage. You'll find yourself reaching for these pieces again and again, and like these friends, you will find, piece by piece, how miracles are everywhere, beginning with you."

—JEANETTE THOMASON, OWNER/OPERATOR, WHITESTONE
PUBLISHING: WORDS AND STORIES TO HANG ONTO

"If you have ever wondered if God is real or if a miracle is possible for you, read this book! In *Dear Deb*, Margaret Terry says, 'When faith holds hands with trust, miracles can happen.' This book is a journey of friendship and a journey of faith, and when you take this journey with Margaret, you will meet a woman who has been pursued and captured by God who will never again settle for less."

—RUTH TUTTLE CONARD, PASTOR AND
AUTHOR OF *DESIGNER WOMEN: MADE BY GOD*

dear deb

dear deb

A WOMAN WITH CANCER,
A FRIEND WITH SECRETS, AND THE
LETTERS THAT BECAME THEIR MIRACLE

MARGARET TERRY

THOMAS NELSON
Since 1798

NASHVILLE   DALLAS   MEXICO CITY   RIO DE JANEIRO

Published in Nashville, Tennessee, by Thomas Nelson. Thomas Nelson is a trademark of Thomas Nelson, Inc.

Thomas Nelson, Inc., titles may be purchased in bulk for educational, business, fund-raising, or sales promotional use. For information, please e-mail SpecialMarkets@ThomasNelson.com.

Quotations from the children's book in the letter "A New Story" are from Christopher Paul Curtis's *The Watsons Go to Birmingham—1963* (New York: Random House, 1995).

Unless otherwise noted, Scripture quotations are taken from the HOLY BIBLE: NEW INTERNATIONAL VERSION®, NIV®. © 1973, 1978, 1984, 2011 by Biblica, Inc.™ Used by permission of Zondervan. All rights reserved worldwide. www.Zondervan.com

Scripture quotations in the following letters are from the 1984 edition of the New International Version: "Rich," "God Is Off-the-Wall," "A Life Saver Day," "Shopping Lessons," "Delightful," "Better Than Gumballs," "'Too Much Love?," "Red Jacket Guy," and "Going Home."

Scripture quotations marked KJV are from the King James Version.

Library of Congress Cataloging-in-Publication Data

Terry, Margaret, 1952-
  Dear Deb : a woman with cancer, a friend with secrets, and the letters that became their miracle / by Margaret Terry.
      p. cm.
  Includes bibliographical references and index.
  ISBN 978-1-4002-0437-3 (alk. paper)
1. Christian life. I. Title.
  BV4515.3.T47 2012
  248.8′6--dc23

                    2012016248

Printed in the United States of America

12 13 14 15 16 QG 6 5 4 3 2 1

Author Note

We do not see things as they are.
We see them as we are.

—Anaïs Nin

The stories in these letters are real events that occurred in my life. Outside my family, a few names and details have been changed to protect the privacy of those mentioned. Many people have asked me how I remember so much from my past. There's no simple answer to that except to say if memory is a way our heart holds on to things we cherish or things we need, my heart was crowded. Once I opened the door to the past, a few memories jumped out like a jack-in-the-box excited to see the light of day; others wanted to stay put, and I had to chip away at their hiding place like a miner. I am grateful to my sisters, Lisa and Deborah, to my dad and my cousin Geri, who confirmed many childhood stories. They helped me stay as true as possible to time lines and dialogue while respecting that each of our perspectives was unique.

*For Deb, and all the Debs who
believe in miracles . . .*

We are each of us angels with only one wing;
and we can only fly by embracing one another.
—Luciano de Crescenzo

Contents

The Inspiration

"I'm going to have a miracle."

I strained to hear her words, thin whispered sounds she wheezed with each ragged breath. "I need you to help me believe it."

Deb didn't say what the miracle would be, only that she was certain she would have one. We were sitting with a circle of friends who had met in the church nursery to pray with her after her recent diagnosis of stage 4 inoperable lung cancer. We all knew what inoperable meant but didn't dare speak it aloud. Inoperable meant terminal, a word that didn't belong in a nursery, a word that didn't exist when we were children singing, *"Sticks and stones will break my bones, but words will never hurt me."* Deb had beaten breast cancer a few years earlier. "Survivor" was the label she had been wearing until that day when "terminal" tried to take its place.

I was surprised to be invited to pray for her. You can

count on me to make meals when someone's sick; or if you need help planning a fund-raiser, I'm there with marketing ideas and a trunk full of donations. But praying aloud in a group makes me uncomfortable. Plus I wasn't that close to Deb. She was a church friend I'd known for six years, someone who planned retreats and study groups, a can-do gal who rolled up her sleeves to help even when she wasn't asked. I knew she loved red wine, Motown, and the Buffalo Sabres, but outside church Deb and I didn't social-ize. We didn't talk on the phone, meet for coffee, or go to the movies. I'm not sure why this happens in churches. We hug the same people every Sunday for years, we watch their children grow, and we share their trials and joys, yet for some reason we limit our relationship to church friend. Maybe that's why I decided to join the group to pray for her. She was sick, and I thought she might need a better friend than the one I'd been.

After we finished praying, Deb declined all offers to make meals, clean her house, or run errands. When we asked what we could do for her, she said, "Send me encouraging words, and believe in my miracle."

Encouraging words was something I could do.

I've been a storyteller since I was six years old, when my mother had her first series of electroshock therapy treatments. I made up stories to keep my sisters quiet while Mom slept. She slept a lot. Sleep was her refuge, her only sanctuary, from the depression battles she lost no matter how many electro currents assaulted her body. In those days we didn't have books in our house, but we had the Sears catalog filled with pictures of smiling children dressed for every occasion. My sisters and I would snuggle shoulder to shoulder on our big, old, weathered couch and shuffle those catalog pages back and forth until we found the right shoes with matching purses to wear on our couch adventures. We could travel to faraway lands, with my imagination the navigator and my sisters a loyal crew who hungered for magic as much as I did.

The first day I sat down to write Deb, I struggled with finding words other than "I believe in your miracle." What could I say that was encouraging when Deb's doctors weren't? For ten days, I e-mailed Pollyanna snippets that sounded hollow, my words echoing my lack of faith in her miracle.

The day Deb received the news she had a brain tumor that had to be removed before her lung treatments could start, I felt dizzy thinking about how she'd stay hopeful with two cancers to fight. I knew Deb was strong. She was tall and athletic, played on a women's hockey team. She was also a woman of faith and could fight this battle mentally and physically, but cancer in her brain *and* lungs had to be terrifying.

That's when my letters changed.

I didn't know how it felt to have cancer, but I knew about fear. I thought of all the times I was afraid of things out of my control, things I might have shared with Deb if we had been closer friends or if we'd had more time. So I began to tell her. I wrote about my divorce and how I didn't see it coming. I wrote about getting caught shoplifting and about the best dancer I knew, who was a man with no legs. When Deb responded, "No matter how sick I feel, your letters give me something to look forward to," I kept writing. She was too sick to eat, but not too sick to read. Deb's illness gave me the chance to press my face against the window of my life, and what I saw was startling—I saw miracles that had been waiting for me to give them a voice.

Deb began sharing her letters with friends and family, and the letters took flight. In three months, hundreds of people from seven countries were reading the Dear Deb letters every day. Strangers wrote who were struggling with their lives yet refused to let go of hope. Some talked about their own miracles; others yearned for one.

As I wrote, I was aware that Deb and I were building a bridge we would never cross. Bridges to intimacy take years. I knew I was gaining something and losing it at the same time. I was riding the crest of a wave that would crash when it reached the shore, but I kept riding it, riding and hoping that as long as I kept writing, Deb would keep living. In six months I wrote 102 letters to her. I only saw her three times during those six months, but a lifetime passed between us that created a bond that defied time. She refused to consider how much time she had—instead she concentrated on living, and she was busy making plans right up until the moment she took her last breath.

Deb was fifty-five years old when she died.

What follows are fifty-five Dear Deb letters, one for each year she graced this world with her beautiful presence.

The Letters

Index of Letters

Real Family

Dear Deb,

"Is your dad a *real* dad, Mom?" Patrick stood beside me in front of the sink in the thimble-sized bathroom. He leaned over the counter and pressed his nose against the mirror.

"Yes, he's a real dad." I smiled at him in the mirror, batting my eyelashes to check if my mascara had set. I had applied waterproof just in case tears ambushed me when I saw him. "He's *my* dad, honey." My sons knew my sisters and my mom, who had visited us in Minnesota over the years, but they had never met my father.

That fall, Dad had decided it was time to meet his grandsons. Michael and Patrick were eleven and eight and didn't know much about him other than his name was Donald, his high school friends called him Ducky, and he lived in Ohio. There had been promises to visit over the years, but we never made it happen. The letters and cards

I sent with school pictures and family photos were as close as my dad wanted to be to me. Beyond updating my address book, I didn't do much to nurture a relationship with him either. He was my real dad, but we hadn't had a real relationship since I left home in my early twenties. When I announced his visit, Michael and Patrick acted like Christmas was on its way instead of my dad. They had a grandfather! They loved the mystery of the stranger who fathered me suddenly appearing at our doorstep.

Dad had aged well. He was more handsome than in the seventies, when people mistook him for Sonny Bono. His hair was peppered with white, but thick and lush as a rich carpet. He wore a soft, cream, V-neck sweater with a pink collared shirt underneath and gray flannel pants. No wonder his friends called him Dapper Don.

The boys had been playing Capture the Flag in the yard, waiting for his arrival. By the time they tumbled into the kitchen, Patrick's new khaki pants were covered in grass stains and Michael's pale blue button-down shirt was flecked with prickly pine needles. Their eyes gleamed as they stood in front of us with their eager smiles. I wanted to throw my arms around them and exclaim, *"Look, Daddy! Look what I made! Aren't they beautiful?"*

But I stopped myself. I wasn't going to let Dad see how much I cared about him being proud of me. After a twenty-year absence in my life, I was surprised I cared at all.

I stood in between Michael and Patrick and draped an arm over each of their shoulders. "Dad, this is Michael, and this is Patrick."

Michael stretched his arm out to shake my father's hand. "Hi, Grandpa. I'm Michael," he chirped. I thought my heart would burst out of my chest like a cartoon rocket.

"Oh my gosh . . . oh my . . ." Dad shook Michael's hand and stepped back. He cleared his throat, coughed, and wiped his eyes with the back of his hand. "He looks . . . he looks like . . . *he looks like me* . . . He could have been my twin . . ." Dad held his palm against his heart and sat at the kitchen table. He couldn't stop staring at Michael. "It's uncanny," he said, shaking his head back and forth. "I just can't believe the resemblance."

Michael sat facing him. "You looked like *me* when you were eleven, Grandpa?"

"I sure did, pal! I'm gonna send you a picture of me in grade school so you can see for yourself." Dad leaned back and placed his hands flat on the table.

Michael imitated him, peering over his own hands to see if their hands looked alike too. I felt a curtain lift as I remembered moments of my childhood. Dad's strong, masculine hands, always immaculate, nails trimmed evenly. Hands that swung me in circles playing airplane, hands that showed me how to catch a ball, hands that clapped the loudest when I bowed at the curtain calls of my high school plays.

I felt a powerful urge to rush over and stand between my son and father at the table. My desire to grab both their hands and hang on made me feel like I was being carried by a current strong enough to launch me over a waterfall. I yearned to know what it would feel like to touch them both at the same time, to be connected and to feel what other families felt, families who celebrated holidays together, families who learned forgiveness and who were unafraid of their pasts.

But I didn't move. A nerve twitched under my eye. I held my finger on the pulse until it stopped.

Patrick joined them at the table. "I'm glad you're here, Grandpa." He pulled on his wrists like he was playing tug of war with his arms.

"Hey, Grandpa?" Michael asked. "I've got a question for you!"

"OK, kiddo," Dad answered. He leaned forward. "Shoot."

"How come you took so long to meet us? I'm eleven now, you know." He picked a pine needle off his sleeve and flicked it on the floor.

"We-e-e-ell, now. I guess that's the million-dollar question, Michael!" Dad heaved a great sigh and leaned back. "It's a *very* good question, Michael . . . very good." He exhaled a whistle with no tune and looked at me for help.

I shrugged my shoulders. What could I say to help him when I didn't know why he wasn't in my life? I had asked him many times to come to Minnesota to meet my sons, but it had been his choice to stay away.

"Grandpa?" Michael tapped Dad's hand with his forefinger. "Why didn't you come here before?"

"The truth is . . ." Dad cleared his throat. "The truth is . . . I don't have an answer to that, Michael. I really don't know why it has taken me so long to come here and meet you." He hung his head low and stared at his lap.

Patrick and Michael studied him, the father of my childhood who was once a boy who looked like them.

Dad peered up at them, his eyes misted. "But now that I'm here, I'm hoping I can be a part of your family." He grinned a boyish grin. "Starting right now, right here if you'll let me."

Michael stood up and beamed. "You *are* our family, Grandpa. Jeez . . . you're my mom's dad!"

"Yeah," Patrick echoed. "You're our mom's dad! You're family already."

They threw themselves on him and hugged him shamelessly.

They loved him because he was family.

And they loved him because he was there.

"For where your treasure is, there
your heart will be also."
—Matthew 6:21

Rich

Dear Deb,

    I was ten years old the first time I felt rich. I found a five-dollar bill on a neighbor's lawn on my way to school. The familiar blue [Canadian] note lay flat as wallpaper against the lush, dew-covered grass. April showers had prevented us from exploring our new neighborhood, but with the sun shining its glory that morning, the whole street sang with more shades of green than the Amazon. I stood over that little blue rectangle that glowed brighter than a pot of gold, and Queen Elizabeth stared up at me. I couldn't believe my luck—I was rich.

    The bill was so wet I was tempted to wring it out like a sopping facecloth, but I didn't want to risk tearing it. Five dollars was a king's ransom in 1962; I'd never had a whole five dollars to myself. With great care I peeled it off the lawn, folded it in half, and slid it into my pocket where it would be safe. When I reached the end of my block, I panicked. *What if it dries folded and I can't unstick it?* I whipped it out and tried to dry it. I blew on it until I started feeling faint. Then I dabbed it over my heavy woolen kilt, hoping the wool would blot away the dampness. That didn't work, so I raised my arm high above my head and let it wave like a race car pennant. It flapped and flapped as I ran, but when I reached my school, it still felt damp as an old kitchen sponge that refuses to dry.

Just before I entered my classroom, I had a brilliant idea. I could protect it and dry it at the same time if I tucked it inside the waistband of my skirt. I slid it between my fingers first to iron out any creases before I pressed it flat against my tummy. It felt cool and clammy against my skin. I wondered if this was what rich felt like.

Miss Anderson rattled on about a new concept for a science fair while I fantasized about all the ways I could spend my newfound wealth. I had wanted a Barbie doll FOREVER, but Mom said they were too expensive and with three younger sisters to play with, I didn't need a doll. A real Barbie cost $3.99. Even my sister, who was Barbie's namesake, didn't have a *real* Barbie doll. She pretended her cheaper imitation was a real Barbie, and we'd let her think she was, even though we all knew the difference. With my five dollars, I had enough money to take the bus downtown to Woolworth's, get my favorite Barbie wearing the striped bathing suit, plus buy a bag of cheese popcorn I could eat all by myself on the bus ride home.

As I dreamed about Barbie and licking cheesy popcorn powder off my fingers, I started feeling all sweaty. I swiped a few salty drops that trickled down the back of my neck and dried my hand on my skirt. I wondered what Mom would do with five extra dollars. Would she buy food? Or would she slip it in the envelope on the top of the fridge, that was for emergencies? I didn't know how much an emergency cost, but one time I dragged a kitchen chair close to the fridge so I could reach high enough to peek inside the envelope, and there was forty-three cents. I hoped this time she would use it for food. We had just moved again because she had to choose between paying the rent and buying food. It always happened when Dad stopped living with us. Mom would cry every time she had to cook us porridge for dinner. I kept telling her I loved porridge and didn't care if we had it for breakfast and supper, but it didn't stop her tears. No matter how often we ate porridge or how many stamps we saved and licked into those little books, there was just never enough for both groceries and for us to stay long in one place when Dad wasn't there.

The five dollars was beginning to feel hot as a heating pad against my skin. I pulled it out of my waistband and slipped it into the middle of my math textbook where it would dry clean and flat like the red maple leaves I loved to collect in the fall. After the bell rang, I grabbed my math book and pencils. I had carried that book home a dozen times, but that day the weight of it slowed me down so much I was late getting home to help Mom with dinner. When I entered our dim hallway, I did what I always did when we first moved to a new house. I looked for my dad's shoes. When I didn't see them, I felt that familiar pinch in my throat that reminded me I had to act happy even though I was sad. I passed the living room, where the theme song for *I Love Lucy* blasted from the TV. I slipped the five dollars out of my math book, looked at the queen's softened face as she eyed me once more, and I knew what I had to do.

"Mom," I called. "Guess what I found today . . ."

Whether well fed or hungry, I can do
everything through him who gives me strength.
—Philippians 4:12–13

A Tip of the Hat

Dear Deb,

Michael was three weeks old when I bundled him up in his fuzzy polar fleece snowsuit and swaddled him with blankets to walk to our local food market. It was early December, our first winter in Detroit, and it was bitter cold. Winter had announced its arrival with forty-eight hours of icy sleet that shot across Michigan like an arctic jet stream. I worried the few blocks to the market might be more than a new baby could handle, but I couldn't handle another day alone in the house.

The switch from a career selling marketing concepts to changing diapers full-time was harder than I had imagined. When I left Canada for my husband's career, it was a choice I made for love, but with his constant travel, it seemed as if the love had been left behind with my relatives and former life. I was isolated in a Detroit suburb without friends or family. Even though I was thrilled to have a beautiful baby, I felt like the working half of something broken. Walking had been my therapy before giving birth; I counted on it to help me again.

I parked the stroller beside a few grocery carts in the entry way and peeled the heavy blankets away from Michael. He was sound asleep, his forehead damp, cheeks flushed from being overbundled. I untied his creamy knit hat with the little lamb ears that poked out the top, and when I looked at his tiny face, I felt a powerful jolt as my heart slammed against my ribs. It had been happening a few times a day. Sometimes when I was nursing him, sometimes when I pictured the innocence of his tiny face before I fell asleep. It would sneak up on me like a Chinook, those warm, dry winds in the Rockies that could melt the frostiest winter day. I knew I loved my baby, but I felt my heart loved him even more.

There was a line at the butcher counter in back of the store, so I grabbed a number to wait. The homey market smelled like ginger cookies and fresh-cut pine. Jars of home-made jams and chutneys lined the top of the counter, each one hand labeled with a flowery script: *Blueberries from My Yard Jam, Aunt Elsie's Peach Chutney*. Against the side wall, a basket filled with bundles of white pine boughs held a cheery sign: *From our tree to your hearth, $8 per bunch*. Michael slept in the baby carrier attached to the top of the grocery cart. I lay my hand on his lap while I waited. The butcher called "Number 39!" I looked at my number, 42, and yawned.

"Excuse me, madam. How old is that baby?" A tall, elderly man approached me and tipped his hat, a black fedora. His hair was snowy white, combed with a crisp side part. He held a polished wooden cane and wore a knee-length black dress coat with a pearl-gray silk scarf folded at his neck.

"He's three weeks old. This is his first outing." I smiled and slipped off Michael's hat so the kind man could appreciate my son's wispy curls.

"Well, how about that!" he said. "Three whole weeks . . . twenty-one days of breathing, twenty-one days of his little self in this great big world." The man's lips quivered with a smile that lit up his rosy complexion. "I am ninety-two years old, and your boy is the most beautiful thing I have seen today."

His eyes were clear but a muddy gray color, and I wondered if they had twinkled blue at one time.

"Can I touch his face?" He leaned his cane against my cart. "Would you mind?" I watched him struggle to remove his leather gloves and agreed, but kept my hand resting on Michael's lap. He reached toward Michael's face and paused with his arm midair like an artist considering where to place his next brush stroke. Then ever so slowly, he caressed Michael's cheek with a crooked finger. "Perfect." He sighed. Tears streamed from his gray eyes and trailed past his hollow cheeks to dot his silk scarf. "Look at how perfect God made him!" He faced me and, with the same crooked finger, pointed at my chest. "And to think . . . he made him just for you." He tipped his hat once again before he bowed and thanked me for the introduction to my son. My heart did it again . . . *Jolt*.

*And he took the children in his arms, placed
his hands on them and blessed them.*
—Mark 10:16

14

Asking for Change

Dear Deb,

I knew he was going to ask me for money before I reached the door of the coffee shop, and I was ready. I had rehearsed for this very moment. *No, I'm sorry. I don't have any change, but I can buy you breakfast. What do you take in your coffee?* I smiled and looked into his face. His lips were cracked and peeling, his matted hair like boiled wool. The deep furrows under his eyes were blackened with grime, but when he squinted to look up at me I noticed eyes bluer than the Mediterranean Sea. At 6:30 in the morning, the air was sticky from another humid night, and I wondered how this homeless man managed summer on the streets with record high temperatures. I complained every time I left the cool of my air-conditioned home to walk twenty feet to my air-conditioned car.

"Thank you so much, ma'am. I appreciate the offer, but I'm not allowed to eat fast food." He smiled with pointy copper teeth stained dark as the tips of his fingers. "You see, ma'am, there are rules for people like me."

He was so articulate, those blue eyes so clear, I believed him, and I started to get all indignant, wanting to champion this poor guy until he said, "They won't let me eat Tim Horton's or McDonald's, just like they won't let me wear socks in summer." He pointed to his muddied swollen feet stuffed into toeless canvas sneakers. "And they won't allow me to wear gloves in winter, either." He laid his hands on his lap and looked back and forth from hand to hand, examining them with the intensity of a palm reader. I wanted to ask him who "they" were but realized the conversation was over when he didn't look up from his hands. He kept flipping them over and over. Palms up, palms down, palms up, palms down. He stared as though seeing them for the first time.

"Gee, I didn't know they wouldn't let you eat fast food," I said. "I'm so sorry." I felt embarrassed standing there watching while he did the hand-flip thing. I decided to forget my own coffee and hurried back to my car. I didn't give him money or breakfast.

What was wrong with him? I thought. *Why wouldn't he take a coffee and bagel when I offered?* I comforted myself with the fact that at least I'd tried to buy him breakfast. It wasn't my fault the guy was too weird to take it.

When I pulled into my driveway in my oasis of cool that blasted from the car vents like an arctic breeze, it hit me: if he'd accepted the bagel and coffee while he sat cross-legged on the pavement, he wouldn't be able to hold out his paper cup and hope someone would fill it.

Who would give a homeless man money while he sipped a steaming coffee and munched a toasted sesame seed bagel filled with cream cheese? The guy was working. He was doing his job, the only one he knew, and he didn't have the ability to explain that to me.

I turned the key to the oak door on my air-conditioned house and wondered if I would have listened if he had.

Let us not become weary in doing
good, for at the proper time we will
reap a harvest if we do not give up.
—Galatians 6:9

Is It Really Free?

Dear Deb,

One Sunday after ordering my grande nonfat latte at Starbucks, I slid my five-dollar bill across the counter towards the teenaged cashier. She picked it up, and she handed it back to me.

"Have a great morning!" she exclaimed.

I figured she must have been in training and hadn't learned that we pay for our coffees *before* we get them. I didn't want to embarrass her, so I laid the five dollars closer to the cash register and gently reminded her I hadn't paid yet.

"It's on us this morning—enjoy!" She was beaming.

"What do you mean?" I sputtered, thinking I'd heard her wrong. "You mean I don't have to pay you?"

She laughed as she slid my money back toward me. "You won't believe how hard it's been to give people free coffee today. Almost everyone has insisted they pay—so weird. Why won't people just take a gift when it's offered to them?" She shrugged her shoulders and called to the barista: "Grande nonfat latte!"

I headed for my car, clutching my latte, and thought about why it was difficult for me to accept a free coffee. Was it because I was raised to believe "free" means it has no value? Or was it because I think there is no such thing as free, that everything in life has a cost and eventually I'm going to have to pay?

Then I remembered grace. Grace, the gift that has already been paid for, the gift that keeps on giving no matter what I do or who I am. Grace has always been a mystery to me, how it appears when I least expect it. How it sometimes makes me feel unworthy instead of grateful. I sipped my steaming latte and wondered how many free coffees it would take before I could understand a gift like that.

Today I wish you overwhelming grace, Deb.

Set your hope on the grace
to be brought to you.

—1 Peter 1:13

Just Imagine

Dear Deb,

In 1998, my friend Sarah and I were in England on a walking tour. Before we started the six-day guided hike of the Cornwall Coast, we spent a few days sightseeing in London.

"Stop!" I cried over the groan of the cheery double decker bus that had pulled up in front of us. I yanked on Sarah's sleeve. "I have to go back. I forgot to do something, and it's really important!" We had just finished a three-hour tour of Westminster Abbey, the famed seven-hundred-year-old Gothic cathedral in the heart of London. I left the tour tired yet hungry for more. Walking the floor of the Abbey was more exciting than walking the Hollywood Walk of Fame. Bob Hope's and Charlie Chaplin's handprints couldn't compare to standing over the graves of Darwin and Dickens.

"Did you leave your purse in the washroom again?"

Sarah covered her mouth with her hand as the oversized bus coughed toward Big Ben.

"No . . . I have to go back to light a candle for my mom." I'd been lighting candles for Mom in every church I've visited since I was sixteen years old. Sarah was aware of her mood disorders and my roller-coaster relationship with her illness. She had seen me get caught in Mom's web of pain and delusions more than once and how long it took me to free myself from it. For most of my life, I believed I could love her all better. But my love was a bandage that never stuck for long.

The first time I lit a candle for Mom was during a grade twelve field trip to Ste. Anne de Beaupré in Quebec. When the tour guide walked us through the massive copper doors of the town's basilica, she began the tour by pointing out the stained glass windows showering multi-colored stars on the pews. My classmates oohed and aahed over the light spectacle, but my eyes were riveted on the pair of towering stone columns near the entrance. They were adorned with crutches, canes, and braces. Hundreds of them were piled on top of each other, left behind by people who walked away after being healed, each battered walking stick proof of a miracle. I thought if God could help people walk, he might be able to help people be happy. People like my mom.

"Seriously, Sarah . . . I've lit candles and said prayers for Mom everywhere I've ever traveled. From chapels in country villages to St. Peter's in Rome. I even lit one in that manger church in Bethlehem—remember I was there in 1982?" My stomach growled loud enough to hear over the London traffic. We had been on our way to a pub for fish and chips.

"So go back." Sarah plopped down on the bench in front of the bus stop. "I'll wait right here." She patted the bench like it was one of her treasured pets.

"Oh, never mind," I muttered. "Let's go eat." I sat down beside her in the space she had patted. "When I think of all those churches and all those candles, it feels like such a waste now." I looked up at the sky. The sun was making another attempt to worm its way out of the ashen ceiling that had hung over the city since we arrived. "I mean, what difference has it made, Sarah? You know how she is . . ."

Sarah nudged my shoulder with hers. "Have you ever thought about how she'd be if you hadn't?"

Night and day I constantly
remember you in my prayers.
—2 Timothy 1:3

Designer World

Dear Deb,

My heaven was a 1930s summer cabin on Rooney Lake, Wisconsin. The year Patrick turned five, we decided to spend a whole summer there without returning to the city. I was a little nervous being so isolated at the end of a dirt lane, until I started trusting Rooney Lake to show me that fear had no place in its heaven.

One late morning, Patrick stood under a lofty white pine that jutted out over the shoreline of the lake. He stood so close to the trunk, I was thinking he'd befriended another bug like Henry, his small brown spider. Patrick was crushed when Henry had escaped the week before, after he removed the lid on his bug jar to share his hot dog.

I stood at the kitchen window and watched him as I tried to figure out what to make for lunch. I hummed along with John Travolta serenading Olivia, "You're the one that I want . . ." Michael had come in earlier and turned on *Grease* again.

Patrick stepped back about three feet from the tree trunk, placed his hands on his hips, and bowed from side to side like Jane Fonda on an exercise video. He was winking and squinting as though he needed glasses. I made a mental note to make an appointment with our pediatrician for an eye exam when we returned to the city in September. When Patrick stopped swaying, he leaned his head so far back to look at the sky, he fell over.

Patrick brushed himself off and headed back to the tree trunk. He patted it up and down like a policeman frisking a thief. Then he lay on the ground and curled his little body around the base. The tree was older than our 1930s cabin. It would take two or three Patricks to encircle it. At five years old, he had a great connection with nature. He'd sing to the sky, chatter with dirt, and collect anything that moved.

"Mo-o-m . . . come out here, quick!" he called.

"What, honey? I'm making lunch," I yelled out the window.

He jumped up like he had been stung by a wasp. "Come here, Mom . . . you have to come now!"

I ran out the door. "Did you get stung? Did something bite you?" I lifted his T-shirt and checked his back.

"No, Mom." He whipped around to face me. "Nothing bit me." He grinned with his whole face. "But I discovered something!"

I looked at the ground. All I could see was a few

browned pine needles and a twig with a withered cone dangling from its end. "What did you find?"

"Not on the ground, Mom. Look—look at this tree!" He reached out and stroked the trunk.

"What about it?" The trunk was straight and tall with branches starting about twenty feet off the ground. I noticed a couple of knots, a bald spot where some critter had probably gnawed a bit of bark, and a few red ants crawling around with eggy-type things in their mouths.

"Oh, wow," I said. "Red ants. I hope they don't bite."

Patrick rolled his eyes. "No, Mom. Not the ants. Just look at the tree . . . all of it." He lay down again. "Come here and lie down beside me. I'll show you how."

The ground felt cool in the shade of that giant tree. I stirred the sandy soil around with my big toe to make sure there were no serious bugs or anything prickly that might give me a rash. I worried about ticks. I lay close to Patrick, and when I turned to look at him, our noses almost touched. A few sun freckles peppered his forehead. I wanted to kiss them.

"Look up at the tree, Mom . . . then look at the sky at the same time. You can do it." He pointed upwards.

The tree looked taller than a New York City skyscraper from that perspective. I couldn't see its peak. The sky was painted with wispy clouds; beams of brilliant turquoise shone through the clusters of pine boughs. I wished I were an eagle soaring overhead to see my lake and the tip of the tree with its eyes. I wondered if God had the same view as an eagle, and I smiled at the thought of it.

Patrick squeezed my hand and snuggled closer. "Mom," he sighed, "don't you just love how God decorated the earth?"

God saw all that he had made,
and it was very good.

—Genesis 1:31

Letting Go

Dear Deb,

God must have invented swings, because when I learned to pump I felt like I was Queen of the World! That weathered plank suspended by two rusty chains cradled my hopes to reach the sky. For a few magic moments I could surrender to the rush of the wind caressing my face; I could control how fast, how high. I could pump with my eyes open to race against the person swinging beside me, or I could pump with my eyes closed and pretend I was flying through a cloud.

Sometimes I'd watch other kids swing high as the cross bar before letting go and jumping into the great nothing. They'd open their arms wide as though they were reaching for someone to catch them, but the only thing most of them caught was a faceful of dirt. I wanted to be like them, to let go and fly for those few precious seconds, but no matter how much I wanted to let go, something told me I wasn't a jumper. I needed to control where I was going. And I needed to control where I'd end up, which meant the same practiced stop by dragging my feet in the dust.

Many times in my life, I've dragged my feet in the dust and missed an opportunity to feel the freedom of letting go. It's taken me years to learn I don't have to be in charge. Fortunately, faith is a patient teacher. Faith has taught me that no matter how much I want to control where I end up, the control isn't mine to have. Faith has helped me learn to let go of the chains and open my arms wide to embrace life when I do.

It is for freedom that Christ has set us free.

—Galatians 5:1

Lucky

Dear Deb,

When the phone rings at dinnertime, I rarely answer because it's usually someone who wants to give me either a free Bahamas cruise or an aluminum siding appraisal. But a few weeks ago, after the fourth ring, something told me to stop chopping onions and pick up the phone. It was my cousin Geri. We only see each other during holidays when she visits and stays overnight. I love her visits because we end up screaming/laughing about our childhood antics. Geri was the nerviest kid I knew. She taught me everything I knew about sex, showed me how to sneak into the movies and stood up to adults when they were being unfair to children and animals. She still stands tall for the underdog.

"Hi Margie." She sighed. "It's me." A longer sigh, which made me brace myself for bad news. "I just had to call to tell you about Lucky." She started to sob.

Lucky was a scrawny black cat that had shown up on her back porch four years earlier. He meowed his little heart out for days until Geri fed him. She left him food and water for weeks and watched him from behind closed doors until he stopped fleeing at the sight of her. She took digital pictures of him and posted them in her neighborhood in case he had an owner, even though his protruding bones told her he was alone, like her.

"I don't want people to think I'm one of those weird single ladies who feed the neighborhood cats," she said.

Turned out Lucky was from the neighborhood but had been abandoned months earlier by a family who had left him behind when they moved out of town. It was just like Geri to name him Lucky.

After inviting him into her home and loving him for four years, Lucky had a stroke in the middle of the night. The vet had no medical explanation. He said it just sometimes happens with strays—nature. Geri was convinced it was because Lucky never got over being left behind by the family he loved, that he had permanent scars from living through a cold winter alone.

I remember when she first found him and she said she didn't want to keep him. "Animals make you love them; then they die and break your heart," she said.

No matter what caused Lucky's stroke, I believe it's true that some animals pick their owners. Lucky helped Geri remember that loving is always worth the risk. I think he picked her because he knew she had a heart worth breaking.

"Blessed are the pure in heart."

—Matthew 5:8

The Sweetness of Lemons

Dear Deb,

Mom was a better baker than Betty Crocker. One frosty morning I woke with the scent of lemons, their sweetness permeating my room as if someone had bottled their essence and sprayed it over my bed.

I tiptoed downstairs and stopped on the landing. A quiet lived in our house on the mornings my younger sisters slept later than me. Every time I sensed its presence, I paused, hoping to make friends with it, but it never stayed long enough for me to really get to know it. It was a different quiet than waking up in the middle of the night. Even though I felt my sister Barbie's warmth next to me in the bed we shared, middle-of-the-night quiet made me feel alone in the dark no matter where we lived.

When I reached the kitchen, the hardwood floor was toasty under my feet, and the air tasted sweet as sugar cookies. Three pie plates lined with golden-edged crusts were cooling on wire racks on the kitchen counter. Clumps of leftover dough on the flour-dusted table waited to be transformed into tiny half-moon turnovers, a treasure I wouldn't have to share with my sisters if I worked fast.

"Can I help you, Mom?" I hugged the kitchen doorway. I was wearing my lilac baby dolls hemmed with fat lacey ruffles that stuck out like a crinoline on my scrawny legs.

Mom turned to look at me as she stirred the sunny lemon curd bubbling on the stove. Two flour fingerprints powdered her cheek. "Why don't you get a cookie tray and make some raspberry jam turnovers for you and your sisters?" She smiled. She lifted a glass measuring cup to eye level to ensure she had the exact amount of sugar. "Mrs. Wentworth has to have some tests at the hospital, so I thought I'd make her a lemon pie. It's her favorite." Her eyes sparkled, and her newly cropped hair bobbed all shiny and curly. She was wearing her favorite cherry lipstick, Desire. Mom said the right lipstick was the key to real beauty, and a smart woman wears the right shade at all times.

Mom often baked cookies and pies for our neighbors or families at church who were sick or lost their jobs. "There are always people who have less than us who need help. Always remember that. No matter how bad you think you have it, someone out there has it worse." Mom repeated those same words each time we walked to our neighbors', loaded up with her home-baked goodwill, my arms straining with the weight of her generosity. The words of wisdom she dished out every time she baked were the nearest thing to real affection she could offer. I drank them in and wrote them on my heart to use throughout my life.

Gracious words promote instruction.

—Proverbs 16:21

God Is Off-the-Wall

Dear Deb,

Sunday was my least favorite day of the week when we spent summers in northern Ontario with my grandma. My sisters and I had to shed our bathing suits and flip-flops for hats and dresses to drive eight miles of winding back roads to St. Anne's Catholic Church in Mactier. Every Sunday we argued about who would get the window and whose sweaty shoulders would graze our own before the four of us piled into the backseat of Grandma's faded blue Chevy. We'd sit in stony silence while Grandma listened to Billy Graham's *Hour of Decision*. She'd thump her brakes for every hollow on the old road and rev her engine for each incline. Bouncing around in the backseat after a twelve-hour communion fast was torture.

One steamy Sunday morning, I lay in bed doubled over with stomach cramps. "I can't get up," I moaned as Mom helped my sister Donna button up her dress. "I'll throw up in Grandma's car again if you make me go, Mom." I pulled the cotton sheet over my head.

Mom placed her palm on my forehead. "Well, you do feel clammy—maybe you should stay in bed and go back to sleep." She tucked my blankets tight as a straitjacket. "You are not to leave the cottage under any circumstances. Aunt Nell and Uncle Bill are at the house next door but they're still sleeping. Don't bother them unless it's an emergency."

As soon as Grandma's car left the gravel drive, I counted to one hundred and hopped out of bed. I peeled off my pajamas, put on some shorts, and slipped into my new aquamarine flip-flops.

The screen door squawked loud as a peacock when it scraped over the threshold swollen from a week of rain. It breezed behind me, anxious to slap against its frame. I pirouetted just in time to catch it before it slammed shut. I didn't dare wake anyone up.

I stepped onto the granite rock shelf that ran the length of the cottage, wide as a porch. The rock was rippled with charcoal ribbons and dusted with silver glitter that sparkled brilliant as diamond chips in the sun. I blinked to adjust my eyes and tried to focus on the swing hanging by two thick ropes from the colossal arm of the oak in front of me. The swing was the only place up north where I could be alone. The seat was a single wooden plank with a dip in the center smooth as glass, the ropes so long I could pump high enough to flick leaves off a branch with my bare toes. I fit into that dip as though it was a part of me, a part I yearned for when we returned to the city.

But I could swing anytime. Today would be the first time I could walk the path to the lake alone!

The path was a four-foot-wide lane that curved for three hundred feet through the dense woods behind the cottage. The trees that lined either side were so high it hurt your neck to try to find their crowns, the woods so thick and wild that even on the brightest summer days, the path was rampant with dark shadows.

There were rules for walking the path if you walked alone.

The first rule was to carry a stick to whack the bushes to scare wild animals. Lynx, black bears, and timber wolves shared our woods. When Grandma walked the path alone we could hear her all the way down at the lake. She wielded her stick like a machete, bashing tree trunks and undergrowth like she was cutting a path through the jungle. She bashed and she warbled "The Bonnie Banks of Loch Lomond" until she reached the boathouse at the path's end.

Uncle Bill said she didn't need the stick.

The other rule for walking the path was the same as crossing a busy street.

Walk, don't run.

Gnarly tree roots that sprang up through the soft soil in the night were as hungry for prey as newly spun webs.

I had never walked the path by myself because Mom had her own rule: *Never go down the path alone.*

Before I headed down, I paused to scan for anything slithery on the surface. When nothing moved I took a few tentative steps, looking from side to side, and then I stopped.

The woods were alive with sound, as if I had entered an auditorium in the middle of a concert. The drumming of a woodpecker high above me, a screeching crow and the flap of wings, the whirring of an outboard motor on the lake below. I closed my eyes to absorb my outdoor symphony and was surprised to find something in the middle of it.

The quiet.

It lay between the chirping and rustling leaves. Was this the same quiet that kept me company when I pumped high in the sky on a swing? Was it the one that embraced me when the light of dawn woke me earlier than my sisters? I squeezed my eyes tight and concentrated on shutting out everything around me, straining to hear it, to *know* it.

And I heard it again.

I didn't hear it with my ears. I heard it inside me, like it was my own inside voice reminding me to test my baby sister's bottle on my wrist before I fed her. But it wasn't my voice because it didn't talk like me.

You might be by yourself, but you're not alone here.

When I opened my eyes, the path beckoned, and the quiet murmured again.

Fly.

I stretched my arms out airplane-style and tore down the path, my flip-flops buffeting my soles. I leapt over roots, holes, and crevices, my eyes sharp as Superman's. I slapped the birch carved with my initials and stung my palm, but I didn't care. This was better than pumping on the swing!

I would have made it all the way to the boathouse if I hadn't heard a branch snap and echo across my path.

The first thing I thought of was Uncle Bill's wild boar. A few weeks earlier, he heard grunting and growling from the path when he walked down to the lake to fish after work. I stopped and searched for the biggest stick I could carry, hoping it was stronger than my heart thudding against my ribs. I found a broken limb the size of a baseball bat, but when I swung it against a tree to practice, it smashed to pieces, and I was left holding a hollow baton.

Another branch snapped, closer.

I tried to convince myself it was a squirrel or a fox, but my hammering heart didn't buy it. I reasoned that only something big enough to eat me could cause a crack that loud. I held my breath and tried to recall everything I'd learned about facing an animal bigger than a chipmunk. *Look it in the eye, or lie face down and pretend to be dead? Climb the nearest tree? Scream? Run?*

Running and screaming seemed my best bet, but I was at the halfway point. *Do I run downhill to the lake to stand alone on the dock, or do I run back up to the safety of the house?* Something told me to stand still as a rock. My eyes ached as they strained to search the woods around me.

That's when I saw him.

It wasn't Uncle Bill's wild boar.

It was Uncle Bill.

He was weaving his way through the deep woods a few yards above the shoreline, the back of his blue work shirt the only color in the overgrown foliage. *Where is he going so early on a Sunday, his day to sleep in? Why is he deep in the woods?* There was only one way to find out where he was going, no matter how difficult it would be wearing my new aquamarine flip-flops.

I followed him.

I kept my distance and policed Uncle Bill for a half hour as he wound around huge rock outcroppings and climbed over felled trees. When he bent over to pick up something, I hugged the trunk of a white pine so fast I scraped my cheek on the bark.

"You can come out now, lass," he summoned, his Scottish brogue thicker than Grandma's.

I stepped out from behind the tree and looked down at my feet. My flip-flops were speckled with bits of moss. Two browned pine needles stuck to the top of my foot.

"Where you goin'?" I asked real casual as though he had been walking to his car instead of being deep in the woods.

He scratched the top of his head and flattened his bushy moustache with his thumb and forefinger. "You'll see, wee Margie." He turned his broad shoulders and continued his hike. "Watch where you step now, hen. Come along."

I struggled to keep up. He navigated the woods fleet as a young stag though he was over sixty and not much taller than Grandma. Uncle Bill was a meaty Scotsman who was so strong I was sure he could swim across the Atlantic Ocean. In WWII when his ship was bombed in the English Channel he swam for twenty hours as blood seeped from his shrapnel wounds. He was discovered two days later on the shores of France with no memory of how he got there.

Uncle Bill stopped in a clearing and turned to smile at me. I was trying to think fast in case he asked me why I wasn't sweating in a pew at St. Anne's with Grandma and my sisters.

"Here we are now, love." He pressed his finger to his lips to shush me as he walked around the edge of a small clearing. I stopped to look around. Mounds of trillium plants with their shiny dark green leaves blanketed the area, a blanket that would be white as snow each May when the flowers were in bloom. The ground under my feet was spongy with layers of needles, fallen leaves, and moss. Uncle Bill stood in front of a gigantic felled pine tree blackened from years of rotting in the shady glade. He looked up, and I followed his eyes. The sky was so crowded with trees I couldn't see a speck of sunlight until a breeze lifted the foliage and the dark ceiling became a million miniature lights twinkling through the trees.

I scrambled up the fallen pine tree. It was so high my feet didn't touch the ground when I sat on it. "Why do you come here, Uncle Bill?" I breathed in a sweet, earthy scent that felt like mint on my tongue.

"It's my church, wee Margie," he said, patting his moustache again. It was his war decoration, a memento he grew in honor of his lost companions. "I come here every Sunday while Aunt Nell sleeps in a bit and the rest of you are off to Mactier." He said like it was two words. Mack Teer.

"Did you make this, Uncle Bill? Did you chop down

this tree?" I asked, patting the hollowed husk. I looked up again. Two giant elms on either side of the clearing had grown at an angle toward each other and the higher they reached toward the sky, the closer their embrace. They appeared to hold each other up, a perfect arch over this fallen log. A steeple.

"Och, no." He smiled. "I didn't make it, hen." He looked up at the elm arch. "God made this!" He spread his arms out wide. "God gave me my own church." He bowed low to the ground like a knight in front of King Arthur. "But this is a secret, Margie. You must promise to never tell a soul. Your grandma and your aunt Nell like to think I'm a heathen." He winked and dug in his shirt pocket for a smoke—Sweet Caps, his favorite brand. "Now off with ya, lass. Time for you to get back into your wee bed." He turned and pointed over my head. "The path is behind you over that rise. I took you the roundabout way."

I made a vow to keep Uncle Bill's secret until my dying breath. I flip-flopped over the rise without looking back and picked up speed as the woods began to thin. My stomach had that fluttery feeling, and at first I thought I was hungry until I started to giggle. For some reason, thinking about God *outside* of church made me want to laugh. I had always thought of God as only inside. Inside church, where he was painted on the walls surrounded by heavenly angels with long, flowing manes. But if God had made a church for Uncle Bill in the woods, that must have meant he was there too. And if God was in Uncle Bill's church, that must have meant he could be anywhere.

When I reached the edge of the woods, I slowed

down and kept my eyes peeled on the brush for poison ivy and tangles of grape vine branches. My feet were so slippery I slid out of my flip-flops and landed in a glade of ferns that soaked me with sweet dew, and I couldn't hold it back any longer. I laughed all the way back to the cottage, loud enough for God to hear.

> *Then all the trees of the forest will sing*
> *for joy; they will sing before the LORD.*
> —Psalm 96:12–13

Fish Eyes

Dear Deb,

In the morning stillness, Rooney Lake mirrored the jagged shoreline and puffy clouds that peppered the sky. The only ripples that marred the glassy surface were a few billowing rings left behind by fish sneaking up from the depths to snatch unlucky bugs.

Michael and I had been snorkeling for an hour, hunting for treasure. So far we had found a rusty can of Leinenkugel beer, a pair of hot pink goggles with a broken strap, and two plastic fluorescent green worms on hooks. Michael swam beside me, the fluorescent orange tip of his snorkel cutting a tiny wake across the peaceful lake. His head swung back and forth as he searched the lake floor for more riches. His thick cropped hair flared out in flat little wings under the water. I watched his graceful movements as he propelled himself forward with strong, controlled kicks.

I was feeling waterlogged, ready to head back to the

dock, when Michael grabbed my shoulder. He pointed to the bottom, four feet below us. *What?* I shrugged my shoulders. All I could see were a few moss-covered stones. *That?* I pointed to a small pile of twigs bleached snow white, tree bones left behind by a beaver who had dined on the bark. Michael shook his head. He waved his hand toward his chest, our underwater sign for "Follow me." He dove to the sandy bottom and lay down flat on his back; he summoned me to join him.

I hated diving to the bottom of the lake with the snorkel in my mouth. I always forgot if I was supposed to blow out the air or breathe in the air, and no matter how often I tried, I ended up choking on a lungful of water. I shook my head, but Michael was insistent. He kept waving me down, and I worried he'd run out of breath before I made up my mind. At ten years old he could swim like a fish, but I was sure he couldn't breathe like one. I ripped the snorkel out of my mouth, sucked in as much air as I could hold and held my breath. Michael grabbed my elbow to anchor me on the lake floor.

Look! He pointed to the sky. I looked up at the sky through four feet of water. It was the same sky but different. It looked closer, more reachable somehow. The blue was bluer yet muted at the same time. And the sun seemed to be playing tricks on me with light bouncing from one treetop to another. The edges of the shoreline blurred into the lake, and the lake blurred into the land. I felt like I was inside a painting. Michael watched me take in this new view. He smiled and nodded, giving me the thumbs-up before he jumped to the surface.

"Cool, eh, Mom?" He slid off his goggles and perched them on his forehead. "Doesn't the world look like a weird dream from underwater? It kind of makes you feel safer because you're a part of it all, don't you think?" He dove forward and with powerful strokes headed back to the dock.

I had opened my eyes underwater many times in my life, but I had always looked at what was *in* the water around me or on the bottom in case there was something that might bite me. I had never, ever thought of looking up.

That night I dreamed I was walking along a beach on a tropical island. When I stopped to look down at the clear surf splashing against my feet, I saw a gold coin peeking out of the sand. It looked like it was waving to me. I reached down to pick it up and found another one, solid gold, glistening in the sun. I couldn't believe my luck . . . gold coins! I surveyed the beach, hoping to find someone to tell, "Hey, look what I found! Look . . . gold coins!" But I was alone. The sun was brilliant in the cloudless sky. In front of me and behind me, all I could see were miles and miles of turquoise sea hugging the snowy sand as if an artist had painted two parallel lines with no beginning or end.

*I pray that the eyes of your
heart may be enlightened.*
—Ephesians 1:18

Tea Leaves

Dear Deb,

"Hey, you're not dressed." My friend Sarah headed to the fridge for a glass of water, like every morning. Three times a week, after our children boarded the bus for school, we met at my house for a hike along the Luce Line, an old railway line converted into a walking path. That morning was a crazy scramble. We had slept in, Patrick couldn't find his backpack, and both the boys had almost missed the bus. Plus their dad, who usually left long before them, had stayed to discuss something important with me. When Sarah walked in, I was still wearing my flannel pj's and was glued to a kitchen chair—I hadn't moved since he told me the news.

"We walking today?" Sarah peered at me over her glass. Her soft-blue eyes widened as she awaited my response. I could tell she knew something wasn't right, but she'd wait as long as it took.

"David just asked me for a divorce," I blurted out. My lips were so numb, I was surprised my mouth worked. I couldn't believe I heard my own voice saying those words. I felt drugged. I stretched my legs out to make sure they were mine and stared at my pajamas. They were cherry red, sprinkled with bright-pink hearts, and I could see they matched the top part of me, so they must have been mine, but when I tried to wiggle my toes, they felt as numb as my lips.

"Yeah, right . . . and I just entered the Miss America Pageant." Sarah polished off her water and placed her glass in the sink. "You *are* kidding, aren't you?"

I looked out the window at my backyard, where everything appeared normal. The early autumn sun shaded my Persian Queen geraniums that sat on the picnic table in the center of our stone patio. Normal. A fat squirrel with a bushy tail slipped into a knothole in our maple tree that flanked the boys' play fort. And my neighbor's shih tzu was barking at a Colorado spruce, like he did every morning.

All normal.

For a moment, I thought maybe I had dreamt that he had asked for a divorce.

"He did n-o-o-o-o-t. You're joking," Sarah said, shooing away the air in front of her like it was mosquito season. "You guys are the fun couple. You have the perfect lives . . . come on, Margaret—stop it."

I hugged my knees against my chest and rested my chin on top of them, hoping if I squeezed myself tight enough, I could disappear.

"Margaret . . . talk to me!" Sarah grabbed another glass and poured me some water. She set the glass on the table and plopped down beside me. The table was littered with the normal morning leftovers: a ripped flyer for the school carnival, Patrick's sweat sock with a gaping hole in the heel, Michael's Game Boy, and a box of Alpha-Bits. I picked up a sugary *B* and popped it in my mouth.

I thought I had the perfect life. I married a handsome, successful American and moved into a quiet Midwestern suburb where neighbors shared hot dishes and babysitters. I had two bright, beautiful sons who thrived on the streets of our safe neighborhood.

"Did you two have a fight?" Sarah stretched out her arm and swept the breakfast mess to the side of the table.

I shook my head. "No, there was no fight. We were out for dinner with friends last night. I don't get it . . . I really don't get it, Sarah." I stared at my lap and picked at a brown stain on one of the pink hearts on my pj's. How would I have known this was coming? Our marriage wasn't perfect, but whose was? Plus, we had just spent a long weekend at the cabin to celebrate our fourteenth anniversary. It was early October but warm enough to go skinny-dipping again, something we giggled about every time we snuck au naturel into the lake. We almost drowned from laughing when a fisherman crept up on us, quiet as a loon in his fiberglass skiff. That weekend, we played cribbage, shared candlelight dinners on the deck, and read every night in front of the fire. How could I believe he didn't love me anymore? How could I believe he wanted a divorce?

"I'm not kidding, Sarah. He finished his Grape-Nuts and put his bowl on the kitchen counter while I was frying an egg for myself. He said he had something to tell me, so I turned off the stove and sat right here."

Sarah sat up and covered her mouth with her hand. Her eyes looked like they had just seen a purse snatcher knock an old lady to the ground.

"He said, 'I don't want to be married to you anymore.'" I spit it out in one breath, afraid the words would choke me. "He also said he was going tell the boys after school today and that he was leaving *tonight*." I felt like I was breathing though a straw.

"This is crazy—maybe it's some kind of midlife crisis thing. Maybe he just needs to go buy a sports car or something." She fell back on her chair and crossed her arms as if she had solved the puzzle.

My whole body buzzed. I hadn't felt that way since I took too many diet pills to lose weight in the seventies. "Look at me . . . I'm the star of one of those movies where the wife is the last to know. I just can't believe this." I ran my fingers through my hair, grabbed huge handfuls, and pulled hard.

Sarah reached across the table and gently pried my arms away from my head. "I hate that this is happening to you."

I shook her off. "I can't *believe* this is happening to me. I *won't* believe it. I just won't . . . I won't . . . There must be something I can do!"

I jumped up and started pacing. "Maybe he had a temporary insane moment . . . or maybe *I* did . . . Yes, that must be it. I'm losing it, like my mom . . ." It had always been one of my greatest fears. That I would somehow "catch" it, that I would end up confused and lost in my own mind with an illness that had no cure. I held on to the counter for support and faced Sarah, hoping I'd feel saner. "Maybe my brain had one of those weird synapse things where it thinks something is happening but it's really not. Or maybe it's something I saw on TV or read about in a book that happened to someone else—you know how weird stuff happens—like déjà vu. Or, maybe, just maybe, I heard him wrong." I hoped that was it. I heard him wrong. I made the sign of the cross in a huge, swooping motion and looked skyward. But it never occurred to me to ask God for help. He was like a distant relative I only thought about at Christmas.

Sarah stood up and placed her hands on my shoulders. "Maybe you should call him at work. What if you did hear him wrong, Margaret? Just call him and see. None of this makes any sense."

When his secretary put me through, I felt like I was standing on the edge of a cliff, swaying back and forth, back and forth. I hung on to the phone for dear life and prayed the wind would blow the right way.

He answered the same as always, with the deep, confident voice I had fallen for fifteen years earlier. He sounded like nothing had changed . . . like he hadn't just asked me for a divorce. *I must have heard him wrong! How could he sound so normal if he was serious?*

"Hi. It's me," I managed to squeak out, trying to sound as confident as him.

He didn't answer.

"Hello? . . . Hello? . . . Ummm, honey? Are you there?" I was shaking. The vacuum on the end of the line was so hollow I thought he'd hung up. "Can we talk for a minute about what you said this morning? Were you serious? Are you saying you really want a divorce? Can you come home so we can talk about this? . . . You can't be serious . . ."

Sarah leaned against the kitchen counter, watching me. She smiled and held both hands up with the thumbs-up sign.

He cleared his throat. "I've never been more serious in my life: we're finished. I'm done."

"What do you mean? Why? How? How can we be 'done'? We just had our anniversary. What about the cabin?" I didn't recognize the cartoon voice spilling out of me until I heard the dial tone and realized I was talking to a dead end. I placed the phone on the receiver and fell against the kitchen counter next to Sarah. I picked up his cereal bowl with both hands. The white porcelain was icy cold. I closed my eyes to try to focus and stop shaking. *This can't be happening. This can't be happening* . . . I felt like I was on one of those carnival rides where the floor falls out from under you and you can't do anything to stop it except watch it disappear while everything around you spins faster and faster. I wanted to throw his bowl. Throw it and let it smash all over my hardwood floor . . . run away and let someone else clean up the mess . . . I wished the house would fall on me so I could end up in another world.

But when I opened my eyes, I was still holding his cereal bowl in my hands. I shook the bowl, swishing the leftover Grape-Nuts around in the milk, hoping I could read them like tea leaves, but all I could see was *I don't want to be married to you anymore.*

The LORD *is close to the brokenhearted.*

—Psalm 34:18

Crowning Mary

Dear Deb,

I was thirteen years old when I witnessed my first miracle. Perched in the front row of the choir loft high above the sanctuary of Sacred Heart church, my eyes were fixed on Sister Ignatius in front of me. Sister waved her baton as though she were directing the Mormon Tabernacle Choir instead of twenty high school girls. I ducked when the heavy sleeve of her black habit almost smacked me in the face when she signaled the alto section.

The church was filled to capacity. Everyone had come to celebrate the May Crowning, the annual ceremony that honored the Blessed Virgin and planted hearts with the promise of spring. From my seat high above the crowded pews, I felt the coolness of the spring air perfumed with the scent of lilacs. I watched every head turn their attention to my sister Barbie, who had been selected to place the crown on the statue of Mary. She looked reticent as a child bride as she inched her way down the aisle in a flowy white dress that trailed behind her. The floral crown she cupped in her hands quivered with each tiny step she took toward the altar.

"*Bring flowers of the fairest, bring flowers of the rarest,*" the choir sang as Barbie approached the statue of Mary standing tall in the center of the altar. She hesitated when she reached the wobbly wooden steps that had been placed at Mary's feet. The choir reached the refrain: "*O Mary we crown thee with blossoms today, queen of the angels, queen of the May . . .*" Barbie climbed the three steps, reached up with her hands clasping either side of the crown, and tried to place it on Mary's head.

She was about four inches short of reaching Mary. She tried again. Reaching, reaching high up on her tippy toes, but the floral crown only grazed Mary's lips. I stopped singing and held my breath. Sister Ignatius looked like a mouse had run up her habit. She mouthed, *Keep singing.*

"*O Mary, we crown thee with blossoms today.*"

Barbie tried again but still wasn't close to reaching Mary's head. I searched for my father in the crowd and prayed he'd jump up to help her. I prayed he would stand on that step with her and lift her high enough to crown Mary. I squeezed my eyes shut and kept praying while the choir sang the refrain over and over. "*O Mary, we crown thee with blossoms today . . .*" A few of the girls emphasized *toda-a-a-y.*

When I opened my eyes, Barbie had backed down a step and stood there just staring at the crown in her hands for what felt like an hour. I was sure she could feel hundreds of eyes on her back.

That's when the miracle happened.

Barbie raised her chin, looked at Mary, and said something to her before she walked up to the top step again. She kissed the floral crown, and the church gasped when she threw her arms high like she was jumping up to grab onto a tree branch. Everyone's eyes were still fixed on her as she pirouetted and descended those rickety steps. When she slid into the front pew and sat down, the whole church gasped again. The tiny floral crown laced with lilacs and baby's breath glowed bright as a halo on top of Mary's head.

At the reception after the service, kids surrounded Barbie, throwing questions at her like reporters after a disaster. *How did the crown get on Mary's head? Did you really jump? How did you reach so high up?* Barbie had no answers. "Did you know Mary has blue eyes?" was all she said.

But I knew Barbie didn't jump like everyone thought. She was lifted. From my perch high in the choir loft, I could clearly see the six inches of air between her feet and the top step that lingered like a spirit and held her up until she placed the floral crown on Mary's head.

He will command his angels concerning
you . . . They will lift you up in their hands.
—Psalm 91:11–12

A Life Saver Day

My friend Susan chose to stay at home to raise her four children. When her children were small, Susan's husband traveled a lot on business, gone Monday thru Friday. Susan said she couldn't have survived those days without Life Savers.

Her four children were born within a six-year period. When they were in grade school, she said she felt more like a border collie than a mom. Each weekday morning she would herd the four kids into the kitchen for breakfast and then herd them back to their rooms to get dressed for school. With them so close in age, if one would complain about a tummy ache, the rest would follow until there was a chorus of sick children singing the same tune at the table. There were days when barking was the only thing that worked to get them to school.

On those days Susan would place more than one

crying child on the bus. She would stand in the driveway and wave good-bye feeling so wretched about her barking that as soon as the bus turned the corner, she'd race to the store to buy four rolls of Life Savers. She'd run to their school before morning recess, quietly knock on the classroom door, and ask to see her child in the hallway. "I'm so sorry we had a bad morning," she'd say as she dug deep into her pockets for the candy. She'd tear open the foil top and offer one. "Here, honey—have a Life Saver." She would take the next one herself, and they would laugh if it was the same color as the first. When she hugged them good-bye, she would slip the whole roll into their little hands and say, "You can have this to share with your friends at recess. I love you."

After she delivered all four rolls with the same message, she would drive home ready to tackle the laundry, bed making, and grocery shopping with joy.

Today, Susan is the proud grandmother of fourteen grandchildren. When her children need parenting advice, they call her up and say "Mom, help me . . . I'm having a Life Saver day."

P.S. Happy Mother's Day, Deb—your children are so blessed to have you for a mom.

May she who gave you birth rejoice!
—Proverbs 23:25

A New Story

Dear Deb,

After eight years of carefree summers on Rooney Lake, Michael and Patrick and I had developed a dreamy rhythm at the cabin without video games, computers, and telemarketers. With the lake and woods our summer playground, there was always something new to discover. One year we spent days wading along the pristine shoreline in search of smooth rocks to paint on rainy days. The endless rain felt like monsoon season. To combat cabin fever we painted our rocks with everything from rainbows to ancient Egyptian symbols. We also cocooned and read together.

Many times we read the same books. Our family rule was the book couldn't be discussed until everyone finished it. Sometimes waiting for the last person to finish was harder than waiting for the rain to stop. *Holes* by Louis Sachar was one of those books. Michael and I couldn't wait for Patrick to finish. We were dying to talk about the crazed warden at Camp Green Lake. She mixed rattlesnake venom into her nail polish, for extra sting when she scratched one of the teenaged inmates who were forced to dig holes in the miserable Texas heat.

Patrick was sitting at the kitchen counter, hunched over a bowl of cereal, when he read the last page.

"Well?" I asked. "What did you think?" I was washing our paintbrushes with shampoo. Rivers of peacock blue and blood red spilled down the sides of my old porcelain sink. I looked out the window at the sheets of rain that hadn't stopped for a week. The puddles on our wooded path were big enough for swimming.

Patrick snapped the book shut and fished for the last few Cheerios. "I want to read it again!" He cupped his bowl and gulped the leftover milk. "But I want you to read it to me this time, Mom."

It was the first time Patrick had asked me to read to him since he started reading chapter books on his own. I knew what he really wanted was comfort, and he didn't know how to ask for it. Both the boys suffered in silence after their dad left. They refused to talk about the separation, how they felt, or ask me any questions about the divorce. I struggled to find ways to get a ten-year-old and thirteen-year-old boy to talk about feelings. When I'd make hot chocolate after school with offers to talk or just listen, they would say they were fine and walk away. But I knew they were hurting. Patrick still struggled to get out of bed most mornings, and Michael was quiet and sullen. Super Nintendo was his escape.

Patrick and I eventually agreed on a different book to read aloud, selecting one that neither of us had read. The rain's hypnotic pitter-patter on the cabin roof called for a fire. I stacked the wood and lit it while Patrick burrowed a cozy spot for himself in a corner of the couch. He wrapped his forest green fleece blanket around his shoulders like a shawl. "I'll share my blanket with you, Mom." He patted the spot next to him. I nestled close and opened the book.

"It was so cold that if you spit, the slob would be an ice cube before it hit the ground."

Patrick looked up at me. "Could that really happen, Mom?" His summer buzz cut accentuated his generous cocoa eyes, dark as my dad's. "Did the Watsons live in Alaska or something?"

"Shhhh . . . Listen . . ."

"It was a zillion degrees below zero."

Patrick pulled his blanket up to his chin and wriggled closer to me. Michael walked in dragging his own blanket behind him. "Can I listen too?" he asked. He plopped down at the opposite end of the couch and leaned his back against the overstuffed arm. He pulled his legs up and stretched them out across my lap.

"All of my family sat real close together under a blanket . . . It seemed like the cold automatically made us want to get together and huddle up."

The fire hissed as a few raindrops splashed their way down the chimney. The three of us remained on the couch while I read into the night . . .

"I will provide for you and your children."

—Genesis 50:21

Fear of Falling

Dear Deb,

Everyone danced at my Christmas parties. We danced with our kids, our spouses, and our neighbors. We sashayed around the dining room table, wove conga lines thru my kitchen into the living room, and danced like *The Big Chill* cast while washing dishes at the end of the night.

But no one danced like Jim.

Jim was Sarah's brother, who had his legs amputated at the hip after a tree trimming accident when he was twenty-two years old. At fifty, he was a handsome, rugged mountain man who didn't let anything stop him from doing what he wanted to do. He had just flown himself home for Christmas from Aspen, Colorado, in his own Piper aircraft. Jim loved to fly. And he loved to dance.

When Bill Haley whooped his countdown, *"One, two, three o'clock, four o'clock rock,"* Jim called, "Hey, Margaret, will your dining table hold me?" He boogied in his wheelchair, swaying his arms and snapping his fingers.

I had just collapsed on the couch from disco fever after the "Last Dance" with Donna Summers. Sarah sat beside me, festive in her red silk dress. She grinned and shrugged her shoulders. "He's a great dancer," she exclaimed. She adored her brother.

Jim wheeled himself to the table and peeled back my white linen cloth. An ancient pine farm table from Quebec, it looked like it had doubled as a work bench with its surface marred by deep scars. I moved a pair of pewter candelabras to the other end of the lengthy table, blowing out the tapers as I set them down. Jim placed the palm of his hand flat on the surface and jiggled it. *"Five, six, seven o'clock, eight o'clock rock,"* Bill Haley roared from the speakers atop my china cabinet. As quick and graceful as a cat hopping up to perch on a windowsill, Jim hoisted himself onto the corner of the table. He made a formidable dance partner propped on the edge. I laughed when he held his arms out and pulled me into his broad chest. "Now we can really dance," he announced. He twirled me away, spinning me like a ballerina.

"We're gonna rock around the clock tonight, we're gonna rock, rock, rock till broad daylight."

With his powerful arms, Jim was easy to follow. I held on tight as we shimmied and jived. He pulled me in, he twirled me out, but after one snazzy spin I almost lost my grip and I wanted to stop.

What if I tripped? How could he catch me? What if I pulled too hard and he fell off the table? What if he let go of my hand and I catapulted across the living room and crashed through my front bay window?

Everyone had gathered around us cheering and clapping to the beat. My dining room had turned into a dance hall.

The next time Jim pulled me into his chest and wrapped his arm around my waist, I pressed my cheek against his and whispered a desperate plea, "Jim, don't let go of me . . . please don't let go. I'll fall and kill myself if you do."

He leaned back a few inches until our noses almost touched, his blue ribbon eyes inviting me closer still. "Trust me," he breathed, his confidence a mighty anchor. "I won't let you go . . . There's *nothing* you can do to make me let go, Margaret." Jim locked me in his embrace. I could feel the steady rise and fall of his chest as his words wrapped their protective coat around me.

"We're gonna rock, gonna rock around the clock tonight."

My dining room vibrated with rock 'n' roll pulsing through the room and guests pounding the hardwood floor. I studied Jim's face. He was a man who flew his own plane and navigated the Rocky Mountains to spend Christmas with his family. He was a man who didn't let anything stop him no matter what happened to him. *Trust me, Margaret . . . There's nothing you can do that'll make me let you go.*

I kissed his cheek and thanked him. Then I remembered how much I love to dance.

The LORD is my strength and my
shield; my heart trusts in him.
—Psalm 28:7

Stones at My Window

Dear Deb,

The day I woke up angry at my hair for being too thick I knew I was in trouble. For months I had felt like I was drowning in a sea of divorce documents; the pages and pages of questions demanded by the court blurred as I tried to read them: *How much do you spend a year on groceries? Babysitters? Entertainment? Long distance phone calls? Gas?*

I was so angry at the growing stack of paperwork I considered putting a match to it, but I knew my lawyer would charge me a bundle for the additional copies she'd have to send me. I didn't like this me who was so angry she couldn't read or balance a checkbook. I missed the old me, the one I could rely on. I forgot how to cook, how to show up on time, and how to smile. The only thing I didn't forget was how to sleep.

My exhaustion feasted on me like a parasite; no

matter how often I slept, my body hungered for more. I didn't know what the date was because time has no meaning when you spend it under the covers—I did know it had been ages since I had walked with Sarah. A brisk walk in the fresh air calmed me right after David left, but something changed once the divorce proceedings started, and I couldn't summon the energy to lace up my hiking boots. My morning routine was enough to send me back to bed: kiss the boys on the cheek; wave to the bus driver; turn off phones; drag myself back to my bedroom; crawl back into bed until Michael and Patrick came home at four o'clock.

One morning, after I snuck back into my cocoon, something woke me out of my stupor. At first I thought it was my bathroom tap. *"Plink, plink. Plinkity plink."* I tried to muffle the sound by kicking my blankets like a two-year-old having a temper tantrum. All that did was make my legs throb. *"Plink, plink plink, plink."* I wrapped my pillow over my head, but when I came up for air, it continued. Had to be another hailstorm, which made me hate Minnesota for the first time since we'd moved here in 1986.

Thunk, thunk. It sounded as big as the hail I had seen two years earlier when I was in the yard playing with the boys. At first we thought it was funny to see the sky raining ping-pong balls—we tried to catch a few until they knocked us on the head. *I should at least get up to see if Michael left his shiny new Huffy ten-speed in the driveway,* I thought. But I didn't have the energy to care about his bike or whether the hail was big enough to smash my bedroom window. I packed my duvet and pillows around me like a shipper wrapping an antique vase with bubble wrap, and I decided to wait it out.

Smaaaack!

That was enough to send my yellow lab, Mozart, into a frenzy. He jumped on the bed and clawed at the covers to hide under them with me.

"Ma-a-a-argaret . . . Margaret. I know you're in there," someone called from outside the house. Mozart stopped clawing and dove off the bed. He barked below my bedroom window as if Charles Manson were trying to break in the house. I threw my blankets off and kicked through the piles of dirty laundry on the floor to find my robe. With the drapes tightly closed, the room was dark as night. I was certain the sky outside would be as murky with the hailstorm, but after I yanked the drapes open to see who was calling me, I almost fell over backwards when the sun pierced my eyes like lightning bolts. Sarah was standing below my window with a pile of stones in her hand. She held her other hand over her eyes to shade them from the glare that bounced off the bleached aluminum siding. "Answer the door!" she called. "I'm not leaving till you do."

Cra-a-a-ack . . .

I ducked as she tossed another one.

"Oops . . . that one was a little big." She laughed. "Uh, sorry . . . Now let me in before I break your window!"

I stepped away from the window and threw myself face first on my bed. *Is she crazy? Can't she tell from the fact that I'm not answering the door that I don't want to see anyone?* I was going to kill her.

"Come on, Margaret . . . You have to let me in. My aim is terrible, and your eaves are going to be plugged with stones if you don't open the door."

I stomped out of the bedroom behind Mozart, who raced past me. I almost tore the front door off its hinges. No one was there. I roared at the front lawn, "I CAN'T BELIEVE YOU THREW STONES AT MY WINDOW!"

Sarah turned the corner sprinting from the backyard and grinned like she had solved the mysteries of the pyramids. "Why not?" She brushed past me. "It worked, didn't it?" She headed toward the kitchen like it was any normal morning and rattled through the cupboards for a glass. "Go get dressed and come walk with me," she called over the water rushing full blast from the tap.

I sat on a kitchen chair and lay my head on the table.

"Co-o-o-ome on . . ." Sarah chided. "You need to walk. It always makes you feel better; you *know* this." She chugged her water.

I didn't know anything anymore. All I wanted to do was go back to bed, and I hated myself for that because I was terrified I was like my mother, who'd slept most of my childhood.

Sarah opened the fridge door. "Got any apples? I'm starving." She rifled through the drawers. I walked over and stood beside her, surprised to see food in there. I wanted to scream, *Who's in charge here?* All my life I was the can-do girl, the leader of the pack, the hostess with the mostest. I was always used to sitting in the driver's seat, and somehow I had ended up in the backseat, sleeping.

Sarah bit into her apple. "M-m-m-m . . . good one."

She smacked her lips. "Nice hair, by the way . . . You get a new do?"

I ran my fingers through my hair. I couldn't remember the last time I took a shower. I looked at my palms to see if there was grease on them, and when I turned over my hands I noticed my nails. My Hot Chili polish was chipped and cracked. I looked up at Sarah and shrugged. A tiny muscle at the corner of my mouth twitched and fluttered. I tried to brush it away with my finger.

Sarah took another bite of her apple and looked at me. "Hey—are you *smiling*?" She offered me a bite. When I shook my head, she said, "You know what? I kind of like you better now that you aren't trying to be so perfect." She tossed the apple core in the sink. "Come on. Go get dressed . . ."

He said to me, ". . . My power is
made perfect in weakness."
—2 Corinthians 12:9

On the Sidewalk

Dear Deb,

A few days ago I watched a girl descend from a city bus while I was stopped at a traffic light. She was an average-looking teen wearing weathered blue jeans with frayed hems that brushed against the sidewalk. She was laughing her head off as she descended, but she was alone. As the bus doors wheezed behind her, she dropped an overstuffed backpack at her feet and turned to watch the bus thunder down the street.

When she looked up, her face was bright with an afterglow smile, the kind you get from a great punch line that takes hold and won't let go. Her hair was swept off her face and tied in a ponytail that fell over her shoulder as she bent down to pick up her heavy pack. She clutched something in her hand and struggled to heave her pack over her shoulder with only one hand. After she managed to thread her arm through the padded strap, I saw what she was holding. It was a small book. A paperback.

Once her backpack was squared on her shoulders, she turned the book to her marked page and started to read. She held it in her open palms like an offering to the sky and she read as she walked, her smile growing with each step.

My traffic light turned green, and I didn't get a chance to see the title that caused this girl to laugh out loud on a bus. I was dying to know what book captivated her so much that she walked and read at the same time. I've known that feeling too. I've known the power of words that could make me laugh for days with the memory of them and words that could transport me through time and space. As I drove home, I saluted the author that captured this young girl's heart, and I smiled in communion with her.

> *When your words came, I ate them; they*
> *were my joy and my heart's delight.*
> —Jeremiah 15:16

In Your Face

Dear Deb,

Today on Facebook I read this post: "Want to find God? Look into the face of the next person you see." It was written by my friend Leonard Sweet, author, preacher, scholar. A man who is passionate about his work, he embraces the wonder and mystery of God with a theologian's mind and a child's heart and asks us to hold hands with him as he follows Jesus. He shares his faith, his life, and his work in his many books and sermons. Lucky for me, he also shares on Facebook. His daily postings are challenging and provocative and meant to be interactive.

My first thought was the next face I would see would be my own when I went upstairs to brush my teeth. Or my black Lab, Viking's, who lay on the floor, curled at my feet. That thought made me laugh so loud, Viking jumped up and barked like someone had rung the doorbell. "Sorry, Viking," I said, which in dog talk translates to

"Come here, baby." He leaned all ninety pounds against my leg and laid his burly black head on my lap. His tail swept back and forth across my oatmeal carpet, painting a path of inky fur. "Viking, is God in there?" I looked into the depths of his dark eyes. He cocked his head and lifted a meaty paw to rest on my knee. I pushed him away before he got the idea to put both front paws on my shoulder, a neat trick Michael taught him.

I walked over to the foyer mirror and looked at my reflection. "Are you in there, God?" Since our eyes are supposed to be the windows to our souls, I looked deep into my own. I figured if God was in me, that's how I'd spot him. All I could see were crater-sized wrinkles filled with sooty smudges. I hadn't washed my face yet.

On my way upstairs to dress for my morning hike, I noticed a picture in the hallway hanging askew. It was a portrait of Patrick at two years old. Dressed in white pants and a white sweatshirt on an all-white background that was the decorating rage twenty years ago, he looked like a little angel enveloped by a sea of white. Above Patrick's portrait was the exact same scene with Michael taken three years earlier when he was two. Michael was facing the camera and poised perfectly on the edge of a wooden toddler chair that had been sprayed white to fade into the white backdrop. An enormous white teddy bear was propped on the floor at his feet. I had kept the white clothes and props and prepaid the photographer with plans of having matching portraits when Patrick turned two.

Except when the time came, Patrick didn't want his picture taken. I rescheduled the sitting three times before the photographer said, "Bring him in today or you'll lose your deposit."

After a promise of a McDonald's Happy Meal, I managed to dress him in the white clothes. When he entered the studio and saw the little toddler chair, he ran over and straddled it. With his back to the camera. A few Skittles convinced him to face the photographer. As soon as he swallowed the last fruity morsel, he ripped off the white sweatshirt and piled it high on his head like a turban. I dressed him again with a promise to visit his favorite park if he would look at the camera and let the nice man take his picture. He said, "OK, Mommy," sat down on the floor behind the chair and faced the camera. He played peekaboo with the photographer, who by that time didn't want to play with anyone.

I ran out of Skittles, and the photographer left to attend to the next client, who had been waiting for us to finish. I was sure I was going to lose my deposit, and I wouldn't have my matching portraits. And then I remembered how every snapshot I had of Patrick, he was doing something goofy. Santa hat pulled down to cover his face. Cereal bowl upside down on his head with milk dripping down his face. He'd do anything to make Michael laugh.

"Patrick, why don't you show us how you want to sit? You don't have to sit exactly like Michael in his picture. I don't care how you sit just as long as we can see your face."

I left him alone in the small windowless studio for a minute. When I returned with the photographer, Patrick had dressed and was sitting sideways on the chair with his face toward the camera. He held the oversized teddy bear on his lap with both his arms around its waist. The bear was upside down. Patrick's chin rested between its fat wooly legs. I nodded, and the photographer started to shoot.

I adjusted his picture and smiled. Patrick hadn't changed. For twenty years he's been fearless in protecting his Patrickness. He's helped me become a better parent by teaching me that my way wasn't always the best way. He's shown me that each of us hears a different tune and that by listening to our own symphony, we can become who we were meant to be.

"For to see your face is like
seeing the face of God."

—Genesis 33:10

The Rock

Dear Deb,

Sister Mary Francis told the fourth grade class that God was everywhere. The class went wild. How could God possibly be *everywhere*?

Questions were hurled at Sister from every corner of the room like a snowball siege, with her alone against the students.

"Is God under my bed?"

"Is he in my closet?"

"In the fridge?"

"Yes, yes, yes," Sister repeated. "God is everywhere." She clasped her tiny hands together in front of her. The open sleeves of her black habit draped below her knees, sleeves big enough for me to crawl inside and hide. Sister calmed the class and gave each of us a turn to suggest a place where God might *not* be. No matter what place anyone suggested, she said the same thing. *God is there too.*

But I knew a place. I was sure God wasn't in my imagination, the place with faraway lands where children ruled and spoke languages only my sisters and I knew. How could God know about that secret place?

When my turn came and Sister Mary Francis asked me to name a place where God couldn't be, I wanted to say, "My imagination," but I had vowed never to tell anyone about those worlds or the special language I shared with my sisters. Instead, I hesitated and answered, "Under the rock."

The class roared. The rock was the most prized spot on the playground. It grew out of the pavement and was big enough to hold two kids on top, standing side by side while we played King of the Castle.

Sister looked at me and smiled. "You are right, Margaret. God is not under the rock."

I couldn't believe it—I had figured out a place where God couldn't be. I'd won! The whole class turned to look at me as Sister continued. "God isn't under the rock," she repeated. "He *is* the rock."

Stumped me for years . . .

Truly he is my rock and my salvation.
—Psalm 62:6

Where's Jesus?

Dear Deb,

I couldn't believe my sons wanted to go to church.

"Come on, Mom—let's go! Let's just try church to see how it feels," Patrick said, as though church were an amusement park he wanted to check out. I kept putting off his request by convincing myself it was a phase, like Power Rangers or Beanie Babies.

He got the idea of going to church from Michael's best friend, Grant. Grant talked about his church all the time. He'd sit at our dinner table, shoveling Kraft Dinner down his throat, and entertain us with stories of all-night church sleepovers with movies, hide-and-seek and Capture the Flag. He kept repeating "fun" when he talked about church, which made me wonder about cults and brainwashing.

I hadn't been to church in over twenty-five years. My childhood church was not *fun*. Sunday mornings, my sisters and I sat still as statues for over an hour, stuffed into crowded pews crawling with baby boomers who eventually grew up like me to challenge what we heard in church. The God of my childhood scared me. The priests chanted things I didn't understand in Latin, and they lectured us in religion class about rules written in stone with hellfire consequences if I disobeyed them. Most Sunday mornings, while feeling faint from fasting, I daydreamed about boys and breakfast. By the time I finished high school, I'd given up any hope of reaching heaven; I accepted that I'd be spending eternity in purgatory, that permanent truck stop for sinners, and I figured I'd have enough friends hanging out with me that heaven wouldn't matter. Some kids dropped out of school. I dropped out of church.

Throughout my life, if the subject of God ever came up, I always said, "Yes, I believe in God. Of course I do." But I only trusted me. I rarely thought about God except when I was at the cabin with my sons. It was hard not to think about God on Rooney Lake. He was the answer to every nature question Michael and Patrick asked that I couldn't answer. *"How can an eagle see fish underwater when he is so high in the sky?"* God. *"How come we can hear the wind in the woods before we feel it?"* God.

After a year of persisting, I said OK to Patrick and agreed to see what church was like even though the whole thing scared me. I worried about meeting the people who went to this church. What if they were all holy rollers with perfect lives? What if they had rules that I had already broken, and what if when they got to know me they wouldn't let me in?

When Sunday arrived, we drove past country estates with white triple rail fences snaking over hilly pastures. I wondered if I might be going to church for me too. Could this be one of those things newly divorced people do in our search for self without a partner? We dye our hair, go on a cruise, or buy a sports car. Some of us go back to church. I considered getting a tattoo of the Eiffel Tower on my thigh until I realized someone other than me might actually see it, and by that time it could look like the Leaning Tower.

Woodridge Church looked like a new brick community center with nothing to indicate it was a church other than the vast parking lot filled to capacity on a Sunday. Grant was waiting at the entrance to greet the boys, and the three of them bounded down a sweeping hallway. Michael called over his shoulder, "See you later, Mom! Grant says we should meet downstairs when it's over. They have donuts!"

Everything about the appearance of the church was different from anything I had ever seen. I felt like a tourist in a foreign land. The sanctuary was a large auditorium that resembled a movie theater with cushioned seats. Instead of an altar there was a stage with an enormous projection screen. I grabbed a seat on the aisle near the back and looked around. There were no statues of the holy family, no tiny candles to light. *Where is the stained glass, the kneelers, the cross? How can a church not have a cross? Where is Jesus?*

Everyone was chatty as they drifted in to fill the auditorium. No one was whispering. They wouldn't have been heard with all the laughing and talking going on. I folded my arms over my chest, feeling like I had made a mistake to come to a church without investigating it. I shook my head. *No cross?*

Even the music was alien. I felt like I was at an Abba concert as I watched five people line up across the stage, holding microphones. They began to sing, and the whole auditorium rose. Everyone sang along to words that appeared on the gigantic screen.

I'd never heard the song before, but there was something familiar about the chorus of voices singing in harmony that made me feel teary. Did I miss my Dad? He'd sung with a barbershop quartet—harmony always reminded me of him. I dug in my purse for a tissue and wiped my eyes. I perked up once the second song began.

"Amazing grace . . ."

Grandma used to sing that song in her warbly soprano when she strolled through her garden.

"How sweet the sound . . ."

I felt it again. That tingle. That déjà vu feeling that says, *I know this.* It wasn't just the song that I knew. It was something else, and it was making my heart race. I looked up at the screen and crumbled.

"That saved a wretch like me . . ."

I'd heard Grandma sing "Amazing Grace" a thousand times. I knew the words by heart. But I had never *seen* them, and had never considered they meant something.

" I once was lost . . ."

Lost? I felt lost in every room in my own house. Lost in the grocery store, lost when I went to bed and when I woke up each morning. I looked around, to my right and to my left. I was lost, and everyone was singing like baseball fans belting out the National Anthem before the game.

My kleenex was sopping by the time the pastor hopped up on the stage.

He told a story about how messy our lives could be, and I felt like he was speaking directly to me. When he started talking about worry, I slunk down in my seat. How could he have known about my worries? Could he have known I was selling my jewelry to buy groceries and gas because my credit cards were over their limits? Did he know about the divorce? I wanted to hide under my seat.

After the service the foyer was alive with families who'd poured out of the auditorium. I scooted by the throngs in a hurry to retrieve the boys and go home. I was stopped by a woman blocking my path with her arm outstretched.

"Hello. I'm Ruth Conard. You must be new here." She gave me one of those two-handed shakes, cupping my hand in both of hers.

I took a step back and pulled my hand away to tuck my hair behind my ears. "Yes, today was my first day." How would she know that? I had slumped down in my seat at the back, desperate not to draw any attention to me.

"I'm one of the associate pastors here, and I make it a point to get to know anyone new." She looked at me with Mother Teresa eyes. We chatted about the service and the band. I told her about Grant and how my sons had bugged me for months to come.

"Would you like to meet for coffee sometime this week?" She smiled as she handed me a business card.

Ruth Conard, Associate Pastor, it said, with the church logo, address and phone number along with her personal cell number. I couldn't believe she had a business card and a cell phone. Church had changed a lot in the last twenty-five years.

> *Jesus . . . cried out, "Yes, you know me,*
> *and you know where I am from."*
>   —John 7:28

Chocolate Soldiers

Dear Deb,

In 1965 when a new mortgage swallowed both my parents' paychecks, Dad charged into Woolworth's five and dime store on a mission. Ten minutes before closing on the night before Easter Sunday, he planned to purchase chocolate eggs, bunnies, and ducks for 70% off retail.

"You won't believe how much I got for five bucks!" Dad waltzed into the kitchen and laid two shopping bags on the table. "This stuff will fill the girls' baskets for sure." He had rushed to the store after work. He was still wearing his blue work shirt and steel-toed boots that smelled like the gooey tar that bubbled on the roads and stuck to our sandals in summer.

After my sisters had gone to bed, I helped Mom assemble the four Easter baskets lined up on the dining room table. I placed two pastel-tinted hard-boiled eggs in each basket and sprinkled jelly beans on top of the bright pink cellophane grass. A few slipped through to rest on the bottom, chewy gems to discover after the last chocolate morsel had been devoured.

Mom emptied the shopping bag with the Woolworth bargains and gasped. "This bunny's broken, Donald . . . and so is this one . . . It doesn't have a head." The clear window on the front of the yellow and pink boxes exposed the damaged chocolate. A hollow duck with a hole in his belly big enough to fit a small plum, a rabbit without feet, a chocolate puppy in pieces and one without a head.

Dad sat in his La-Z-Boy, reading the paper. "It doesn't matter if they're broken. It all tastes the same. What's the difference?" He shook his paper and folded it in half.

"I can't put broken bunnies in their baskets . . . I can't." Mom cried. "How can I make them look special when they are all broken?" She opened a box and removed a bunny that was in two pieces. She held the ears in one hand and the body in the other, then fit them together like a puzzle. She stomped into the kitchen with them in her hand.

Dad and I followed when we heard the whir of her electric mixer. Mom was an incredible baker, but I couldn't imagine how she could fix these.

"Glue." She looked up at us, adding more milk to the powdered sugar.

"We'll fix them with frosting." She stopped whipping the frosting and stuck a wooden spoon into the center of the bowl. The spoon stood upright like a fence post planted in cement. A pot of milk simmered on the stove. "Or we can use hot milk. Chocolate melts, so we can brush the milk on both sides and hold the pieces back together until they harden. Margie, take them out of the boxes and bring the parts in here."

Hours later our kitchen table was covered with candy veneer, a mosaic of chocolate shards and beads of hardened frosting. The patched bunnies and ducks sat on the table leaning against the wall to dry, a row of wounded chocolate soldiers.

"Hey, they look great . . . just like new!" Dad tapped a puppy on the head with the small paintbrush he had used to dip in the hot milk. "A few scars is all, but I'll bet they're stronger now . . . like broken bones that have healed . . . hah!" He grinned and picked up a bunny with its ears reattached. "See . . . look at this guy." He held it up to my face. "All better!"

Mom stepped back from the table to scrutinize the display. She crossed her arms. "They'll have to do, but they're not better, Donald—they look awful with Frankenstein scars and crooked bodies." She took the bunny from his hands and laid it back on the table. "Nothing's the same after it's been broken."

Before I fell asleep that night I concocted a story to convince my sisters the Easter Bunny had an accident, that he tripped on a kid's wagon left on the sidewalk. I wasn't sure if they believed me, but it didn't matter. As they gobbled up chocolate ears, I realized Dad was right. Didn't matter how they looked on the outside. Chocolate was chocolate.

He heals the brokenhearted and
binds up their wounds.
—Psalm 147:3

Snake in the Grass

Dear Deb,

"Snack time!" I called through the screen door. Michael and Patrick were floating near the end of our dock on their surfboard. After another full day packed with water sports and sunshine, they had surrendered to the stillness of the late afternoon.

"Hey, Patrick, let's not answer Mom and pretend we fell asleep on the board."

"OK, Michael." Patrick started to snore louder than Popeye. He stretched his arms out on top of the water like he was practicing the dead man's float. Patrick had turned six that year and was the perfect magician's assistant, eager to follow Michael's instructions without question. One of my favorite lake sounds was the two of them giggling.

We hadn't seen another soul for days, typical on our small Wisconsin lake in mid-August. Most of the cabin owners had packed their families up by the end of July to return to their scheduled lives in the city. There were days when the boys and I played water Frisbee and the baby northern pikes nipping at our ankles were the only reminder we weren't alone on Rooney Lake. We also shared our summer home with the loons, bald eagles, and creatures of the night whose mournful wails were the only sound for miles.

"Come on, you guys. I have cheese and crackers and those raspberries we picked yesterday. Oh, and I made sun tea!" Michael and Patrick revealed their Scottish roots with their love of afternoon tea, but their American genes preferred it iced, which would have sent my grandma running to light altar candles if she were alive.

Snack time was my alone time. My lifeguard duties ended while the boys read, played board games, or occasionally watched a movie. Most days, I took a book and my tea down to our smaller dock, where no jumping was allowed after 5 p.m.

The boys took their tea inside the cabin. I gathered my own icy glass of tea with a fruit plate, my book, and reading glasses. I balanced them in my arms as I maneuvered the eight narrow steps carved into the gradual slope that led to my dock. I was halfway down to the water when I almost stepped on it. A huge black and writhing thing in the middle of the step. My foot hovered over it for a second before I hurled my snack into the air and flew back up the stairs to the safety of our picnic table. I was sure snakes couldn't climb up a table, but wasn't sure how fast they could chase, so I didn't risk running the extra twenty feet to the cabin.

"Michael . . . Michael! Go get the hatchet out of the garage!" I tap-danced barefoot on top of the table better than Fred Astaire danced on the ceiling. "Michael . . . get the hatchet . . . Hurry! Go get it . . . get it and chop it up!"

Michael opened the sliding screen door and popped his head out. He yawned and scratched the back of his head like he had woken from a nap. "What, Mom? We're watching *Indiana Jones,* and we're at the good part." His tongue played with a few cracker crumbs stuck in the corner of his mouth.

He didn't ask why I was dancing on the table. Earlier that summer, I had convinced him there was a bear in our woods six feet away while we ate burgers on the deck. He and Patrick bolted, spilling their burgers and lemonade. Michael wasn't about to be bluffed again.

"There's a gigantic snake on the step. You have to get the hatchet and kill it!" I waved both my arms toward the steps like Billy the Kid emptying a pair of six-guns.

He couldn't have looked more surprised if I had asked him to drown a kitten. "I'm *not* getting the hatchet, Mom." He huffed. At nine years old, Michael had love affairs with small creatures, wanting to rescue them all. The previous winter he'd wept over a snow-capped squirrel shivering on the tip of a branch on the oak tree outside his bedroom window.

"Come oooooooon," I begged. "I'll be stuck on this table if you don't at least go look for me!"

His sense of adventure prevailed even though he scoffed at me as he walked past. He shuffled down the slope to the bottom step and kicked aside my melting ice cubes and a few scattered apple slices. My plastic tumbler half-filled with lake water bobbed on its side next to the dock.

"There's nothing here, Mom . . . nothing on the step but a hunk of lemon from your tea!" He laughed and continued to search the ground. "You must have been seeing things."

What if he was right and it was just a twig from the sweeping birch that shaded the steps? It wouldn't have been the first time a small twig made me scream. I placed my hand on my heart to calm the thudding.

"It was probably a stick snake, Mom." He grinned. "Should I go rescue your cup?" Michael had one foot in the water when he spun his head around so fast, he almost lost his balance. He scooted up the embankment and cried out, "Did you hear that, Mom? Did you?" He slipped behind the base of the birch and was out of sight.

"What? Hear what?" I yelled. I wanted to throw up. I still couldn't see him from my lofty perch atop the table.

"Oh . . . my . . . gosh, Mom! You were right! It *is* a snake . . . a gigantic one . . . aaaaaaaaaaaagh! It's all puffed up and it's hissing at me . . . It's a cobra . . . I didn't know they had cobras in Wisconsin . . . Oh, man, it's so cool. You should see it. Come see, Mom. It's *awesome!*"

Come see it?

In his excitement, he had forgotten about me standing on the table, freaking out like a lunatic. Michael only knew the brave Mom who rescued baby bats, threaded worms on hooks, and peeled flattened mice from traps I had set myself. He knew the mom who camped alone outside the cabin with him in a tiny pup tent no matter how terrified I was that an escaped axe murderer might get us in the night. This was the first time he had seen me show crazy fear.

When the snake stole away into its den in the sandy embankment, Michael headed back up the steps. I had finally sat down on the edge of the table and tried to look unruffled sitting erect with my legs crossed. I smiled at him.

"You're weird, Mom." He shook his head as he walked past me. "What's up with you and snakes anyway?" Without waiting for an answer, he slid the screen door open to join Patrick and finish watching *Indiana Jones*.

"Do not be afraid or terrified . . . for
the Lord your God goes with you."
—Deuteronomy 31:6

Big Girl Words

Dear Deb,

In her book *Traveling Mercies*, Anne Lamott says there are really only two kinds of prayers, *"Help me, help me, help me,"* and *"Thank you, thank you, thank you."* I loved reading that for two reasons:

1. Someone else is as much a drama queen as me.

2. There are times when I am so distraught the only prayer I can utter is *"H-e-l-p!"*

Over the years, I have learned that God doesn't care about how articulate I am. He doesn't judge my pleas, my flowery words of appreciation, or when or where I pray. Instead he cares about what is in my heart. Like my other friends, God wants me to include him in my life. He wants me to talk to him when I am in trouble. He wants to know when I'm joyous and even when I'm grateful for getting the last loaf of twelve-grain bread at my favorite bakery. Nothing in my life is too big for God, and nothing is too small for him, which means on the days I have no words left in me, he listens when I say, *"Help me, help me, help me . . ."*

P.S. I'm praying you feel God hold your hand during your surgery tomorrow, Deb. And that he holds the hand of your surgeon as well.

> *By prayer and petition, with thanksgiving,*
> *present your requests to God.*
> —Philippians 4:6

Shopping Lessons

Dear Deb,

The months following my divorce, I was so angry I had to clamp my jaw shut to prevent the rage from breaking out. Some mornings my ribs felt bruised from trying to hold it in while I slept. It was as though my feelings were prisoners banging against the bars before the riot. I was afraid if I let one word escape, hundreds would follow like the Charge of the Light Brigade, a cavalry of words.

I did all the right things to combat my anger. I joined a gym, found a church and went into therapy. I also spent a lot of time shopping at Target. Target had what I needed: chocolate chip granola bars, extra lengthening mascara, flip-flops with furry leopard straps, and sunglasses. After trying on the tenth pair, I found a pair of tortoiseshell frames that fit my face from what I could see in the four-inch strip of mirror that angled toward me. I removed them to look at the price: $19.99, a bargain. I reached up to feel my own sunglasses perched on top of my head, Ralph Laurens that cost me a whopping two hundred dollars. My first thought was *I could steal these.*

The thought appeared without warning like a mugger in the dark. I tried to push it away but it stood firm, blocking any other thought. *I could steal these.* It was ridiculous. I didn't need them and could well afford the $19.99. I glanced around for security cameras and saw none. Dozens of turnstile racks laden with glittery necklaces and bejeweled headbands towered over me, a perfect screen from employees at the front of the store. I stroked a black velvet choker trimmed with silver skulls that tinkled like fairy bells. I figured if there *were* cameras and anyone was watching, they wouldn't pay attention to a petite, well-dressed forty-eight-year-old with a cart *full* of Suzie Homemaker items.

All of a sudden, I felt my chest tighten. I leaned against my shopping cart and squeezed the sunglasses so hard, I thought they'd break in my hand. What was wrong with me? How could I consider stealing anything? I was the mother of two sons who would be in big trouble if I caught them stealing. I shuddered as the thought became more seductive. *Take them, take them—look what he did to you.* I glanced behind me and from side to side with the cunning of a cat stalking its prey. With that same feline finesse, I unzipped my purse and slipped the sunglasses next to my wallet. My heart was racing. I squared my shoulders and zigzagged my way to the checkout, loading my cart with whatever I could grab before I reached a cashier.

"That'll be $219.79. Will that be on your Target account?" The cashier sounded as though she were talking to me through a tin can.

My stomach was doing cartwheels. "I'm sorry," I croaked. "How much?" *Breathe,* I commanded, *just breathe. If they catch you,* confess. *Say you thought you were putting your own glasses in your purse. They would accept it as an honest mistake from a woman who just spent a small fortune in their store.*

"$219.79," she repeated as she held out her hand. "Ma'am? Will that be on your account or cash?" She yawned.

"Visa, please." I sounded like Minnie Mouse. I had visions of my picture on the front page of the Minneapolis *Star Tribune*: "Divorced Woman Steals Sunglasses to Get Back at Ex-Husband."

After I signed the receipt, I loaded my purchases into my cart and headed toward the exit. Rushing across the threshold, I stepped into the sunshine and felt a wave of calm as soon as I spotted my car. I started to march toward it but was stopped by a hand bigger than a catcher's mitt digging into my shoulder. Radio static beeped and buzzed behind me, and I knew it was from a walkie-talkie before I turned around. I was busted. The white embroidered letters *SECURITY* on his burgundy jacket confirmed it. I felt as though I had fallen overboard in a tsunami. I clutched onto my cart as though it was my life boat.

"Excuse me, ma'am." He couldn't have been more than twenty-two years old with the teeny red bumps peeking out of the fuzz on his upper lip. "You sure you paid for everything you got?" He surveyed the bags in my cart. A customer hurried past us with her head down. I tried to answer him, but nothing came out. He stared at my face and waited with one hand on my cart, the other holding the walkie-talkie close to his mouth.

My brain went into overdrive reaching for words or phrases that might save me. *Anger*. Be angry! It should be easy to dig into that well. "Of *course* I paid for everything!" I huffed. "Do you want to see my receipt?" I jutted my chin out towards him, but instead of staying there all self-righteous, my chin started wagging up and down like a bobblehead doll on a dashboard.

He sighed and tucked the walkie-talkie into his hip holster. "No, I don't need to see your receipt, ma'am." His young eyes looked fatherly. I wondered if he was old enough to have children. "What I need is to see what's in your purse."

Of course Target had hidden cameras. What an idiot I was. There was nothing to do but tell the truth. I held my breath and unzipped my purse. "Omigosh!" I gasped. "How did these get in here? I must have thought they were my own, and I put them in here by mistake!" My voice squeaked like I had inhaled a tank of helium.

He rolled his eyes the same as a weary cop who's heard every excuse in the world for why you were going 30 mph over the speed limit. "Would you like to pay for them or not, ma'am?" He held out his hand.

I placed them in his hand, steered my cart towards my car, and prayed I wouldn't throw up in the parking lot.

P.S. Friends in Minnesota are reading your letters every day now—many have passed them on to their friends and family, who are praying for you and believing in your miracle, Deb—how cool is that!

I am in pain and in distress . . .
O God, protect me.

—Psalm 69:29

Testing the Waters

Dear Deb,

The sun was setting when I arrived at the park; its red glow peeked through the leaves of the tall oaks that dotted the eastern shoreline of the small lake. The baptism looked more like a family picnic than a church event. A half dozen picnic tables were lined end to end in a single row. Floral tablecloths flapped in the wind, and kids grabbed for paper plates when they became airborne. The Tupperware bowls stacked on top of each other and tinfoil-covered cake pans reminded me I was hungry and had missed dinner once again. The whole group seemed to know one another as they laughed, easily sharing jokes and passing the potato salad.

I felt like an intruder. I wanted to turn around and run back to my car. I didn't belong with these people, and the whole *baptism by immersion* thing felt creepy to me. The only reason I was there was because Michael and Patrick were having their first overnight at their father's new condo and I couldn't stand being alone in the house. And I had nowhere else to go.

"Thank you all for joining us tonight for our annual baptism service." Kevin, one of the senior pastors, stood beside a microphone in front of the park's main pavilion. He was holding a half-eaten cheeseburger in his hand. "We're excited to introduce six members of our community who have chosen to be baptized tonight. First, they'll share their stories that brought them to this decision before we all head down to the lake." The amplified announcement sounded alien in the outdoor setting with children squealing "Higher!" as they were being pushed on nearby swings.

Kevin nodded and a stick-thin teenage girl wearing oversized jeans slung below her belly button walked up to the microphone. Her skimpy black tank top accented skin whiter than Snow White's. With the amount of heavy eye makeup painted on her lids, I couldn't tell if her eyes were open or closed. She palmed a thick pile of index cards that made me wonder if I'd be there all night.

"I was addicted to crack and lived on the streets for almost a year," she announced. The microphone whined, and Kevin leaned over to adjust a dial on the amp. She cleared her throat and asked for some water before she continued to read her cards. "My parents kicked me out of the house because I quit school, and I wouldn't quit using drugs. I thought they hated me, so I hated them back. The only thing I had that felt good was getting high, so I pretty much did anything I could to stay high."

I couldn't believe she was telling us about using crack. I thought this was supposed to be a time to talk about how much everyone loved God and why they wanted to get baptized. Wasn't that what church was all about?

"When I got pregnant all I could think of was having an abortion because I was too young to have a baby—I didn't even have a bed for me to sleep in, so how was I gonna get one for a baby?" She hesitated, peering up at us as if she was checking to see if we were listening. I know I was.

I had never heard anyone share such personal things in front of people—secret things I'd never tell.

"But something inside me kept telling me to go home to tell my parents instead." Her voice strengthened as she read from card to card sharing her drug rehabilitation, the birth of her son, and her reunion with her family. A few times she looked away from her notes to smile at the front row. When she finished, a man and a woman stood up to try to stop a toddler who had escaped their grasp. Running up to her barefoot, he squealed, "Mommy, mommy . . . my mommy," as he wrapped his pudgy arms around her knees. She scooped up her son, kissed his shoulder, and blurted out, "Look how beautiful he is—man, I can't wait to get dunked!" She waved at us. "Thank you all for listening to me." She strode towards her family like she had won an Olympic gold medal. I thought she deserved one.

The next person was a father of four. In his mid-thirties with cropped blond hair, he looked like a professional golfer with his Kodak smile and his polo shirt tucked into his perfectly pressed shorts. "My wife has been coming to this church for six years, and I refused to join her because I thought it was her *thing*." His voice was deep and mellow, the kind that could do coffee commercials. "But everything changed when my father died." His face contorted, and he backed away from the mike, clutching his throat. He whimpered an apology, and Kevin rushed forward to steady him. "I was so angry at God for taking my dad I didn't think I could ever forgive him. As a kid, I was taught to thank God for all the good things that happened; after Dad died, I started blaming him for the bad things too."

I had never thought of that. I wondered if I might feel better if I started blaming God. I blamed myself for my divorce and all the other awful things that happened in my life when all along I could have blamed God? He was probably a pro at accepting blame and never let it bother him.

"After a year of taking my anger out on my family and condemning God every chance I got, my wife finally said, 'Maybe it's time you came to church with me. If you need to keep attacking God, why don't you do it in his house instead of ours?'"

Everyone laughed.

Bill walked us through the stages of his healing, sharing stories of reconnecting with a college buddy at church and how it surprised him that he looked forward to Sundays. Then he invited his wife and daughters to stand beside him. The four-year-old who had snowy blond curls like her mother tugged at his hand until he picked her up. The middle two sisters played kick the can with an empty water bottle, and the eldest stood like a sentry beside her mother.

"First, I want to thank my wife for not giving up on me and for getting my sorry butt to church." Wrapping his free arm around her shoulders, he looked into her face so intently my heart skipped a beat. "Secondly"— his voice deepened as he focused on her face—"I want to thank the members of this church for teaching me so much about love. I have always loved my wife and daughters and have tried to be a good dad, but I never, ever imagined I could love them this much." His tears flowed free as a river down his face. "And, that's why I'm here today." He sobbed. "God made me better at loving."

Everyone on the hillside jumped up to applaud and cheer. He wiped his tears on his daughter's T-shirt and kissed his wife as the older girls circled him, clapping along with the rest of us.

After the final story Kevin strode up to the microphone. "Whew!" he exclaimed like he had completed a marathon. "Thank you to everyone who had the courage to stand up here tonight to deliver your testimonies." He paused and bowed his head. "Let's pray."

Kevin prayed, and I kept my eyes closed to concentrate on the rhythm of the waves licking the shoreline as my old church memories poured over me. I felt a yearning for traditions I hadn't thought about for twenty-five years. Dipping my hand into a stone bowl filled with holy water, icy cold no matter how stifling the church was. Genuflecting. Making the sign of the cross. Confession. Communion. There was comfort in those traditions, and there was community to share them with—I missed it all.

When everyone gathered on the sandy shore to

witness the actual baptisms, I stayed in the back on the hill, feeling like an intruder once again. The wind hadn't died down, and the darkening sky threatened rain. I was sure the lake would be freezing, but no one seemed to notice. Kids were acting like any kids at the beach. They were chasing each other, kicking sand, and running in the surf. Teenagers with multi-pierced ears, wild-colored hair, and clothes that would fit Paul Bunyan gathered in groups talking teenage talk. When Kevin walked waist-deep into the lake, struggling against the waves, I wondered how long it would take for his lips to turn blue. "It's really not that bad." He laughed, hugging himself. "Come on in!"

One by one, the six presenters entered that chilly water. Some had friends and family brave the lake with them. When it was Bill's turn, he walked in holding hands with his wife. Just before Kevin leaned him back to immerse him, his oldest daughter, waiting on the shore-line, squealed, "Stop!" She ran into the biting waters and jumped over the waves to join them. I noticed she forgot to take off her sneakers.

The ceremony was simple and quick. A prayer, plug your nose, then dunk. No one complained about the frigid temperature. No one ran for the warmth of blankets and towels. They took their time and hugged the pastors and their family members who had endured the cold waters to stand beside them. Bill threw his arms sky high like my favorite scene from *Rocky* where he finally reaches the top step. They couldn't have celebrated more if they had reached Mount Everest. From my perch on the small hill

facing the shore, I was sure of one thing: I wanted some
of whatever it was that they had.

> *Jesus was baptized too. And as he*
> *was praying, heaven was opened.*
> —Luke 3:21

Away in a Manger

Dear Deb,

In 1982 I moved to Greece to work on the cruise ship *Stella Solaris*. The second week on board, the ship docked in Haifa, a city in northwest Israel overlooking a bay on the Mediterranean Sea. Smart air-conditioned buses idled on the platform outside the security gates, waiting for passengers eager to tour the holy lands. Bethlehem. Jerusalem. Nazareth. Towns where Jesus had walked and lived.

Since the cruise line expected me to experience all the shore excursions, I signed up for the Bethlehem tour. My heart was pounding every second of the two-hour ride through the desert. I couldn't wait to stand on the land where Jesus was born. I couldn't wait to see the manger. When we arrived in Bethlehem, our bus edged its way through narrow lanes crowded with wall-to-wall stalls selling Jesus souvenirs. We almost clipped a table with a menagerie of plastic angels standing at attention under a neon sign that flashed "$1." I shook my head. It had never occurred to me that Bethlehem would succumb to trashy trinkets like Niagara Falls had. Once our bus was past tourist alley, we inched up a steep hill to Manger Square.

Except there was no manger. And no inn. Forty-foot stone walls, a mosque, and rows of tour buses, but no manger. As soon as we disembarked, we were ushered toward the Church of the Nativity, an enormous limestone structure that resembled a fortress. Over the years it had survived invasions, fires, and earthquakes. It had been rebuilt and refurbished so many times it appeared to be a church built on top of an old church, on top of an even older one. Our group lined up outside the main entrance in front of a stone archway called the Door of Humility. It was a tiny rectangular doorway built to prevent horsemen and marauders from entering and looting. Since the first church had been built in 326, people had been ripping off artifacts and chunks of the wall, hoping for a piece of Jesus. The four-foot-high rabbit hole entrance was so small even I had to crouch down to pass through.

The church was cool and dark inside, its lofty walls blanketed with ancient oil paintings. I looked around; still no manger. Instead there was the Grotto of the Nativity beneath the Basilica that enshrined the spot where Jesus was born. In the basement. As I descended the spiral steps that led to the holy cavern, I could feel my face flush. I felt ridiculous. How could I ever think the manger would still exist after almost two thousand years? I was thirty years old, and my desire to see the manger as I pictured it from childhood was just plain silly.

I stood in front of the marble floor and stared at a fourteen-pointed silver star surrounding a single flame that marked the spot where Jesus was born. The Latin inscription engraved in the star read: *Hicde Virgine Maria Jesus Christus Natus Est*, "Here of the Virgin Mary Jesus Christ was born." I closed my eyes and bowed my head. I wanted to say something meaningful. A prayer. Something holy. But more than that, I wanted something to happen. Maybe have a vision. Baby Jesus wrapped in a halo would do it. Or lightning bolts, with angels singing, *"Gloria in excelsis Deo."* But nothing happened. Here I was standing on the very spot where Jesus was born, and I couldn't think of a thing to say.

I returned to the air-conditioned bus feeling disappointed with the tour. The marble floor and the silver star in the grotto felt fake and overdone when what I hoped to find were remnants of the manger of my childhood. As the bus descended the hill away from Manger Square, I lay my head back and remembered Christmas on East 26th Street. I was twelve years old. I could picture the straw roof and miniature rustic timbers that made up the walls of the little manger Mom proudly displayed each year. I recalled baby Jesus swaddled in a tiny cloth lying in a mound of hay and how my sisters and I played house with him and how we lost him that year and Mom yelled, "There'll be no Christmas without Jesus!" And I remembered how we had Christmas even though we hadn't found Jesus yet. Dad decorated the tree. Mom set out platters with sweet baby shrimps and cubes of ham poked with pretzel sticks. We wore matching flannel pajamas and ate dozens of sugary cookies shaped like Christmas trees and laughed at how the green sprinkles dyed our tongues as dark as the Scotch pine lit up in front of us. But what I remembered most was Mom and Dad sitting side by side on the couch, holding hands. We had turned the lamps off so the tree lights would shine like stars in our darkened living room as we danced to the Osmond Brothers' new Christmas album. When "Silent Night" came on, I stopped dancing and looked at my parents. Mom had her head resting on Dad's shoulder, and her eyes looked all dreamy. Dad was singing, "Si-i-lent night, h-o-oly night . . ." and I remember feeling like I was going to cry, and I wasn't sure if it was because I was so happy or if it was because I was so afraid that moment would end.

The angel said to them, "Do not be afraid. I
bring you good news that will cause great joy."
—Luke 2:10

The List

Dear Deb,

My friend Karen offered me a challenge last spring while we were on a brisk walk: "At the end of each day, let's write down five things we're grateful for—nothing obvious like our kids or our house. Let's be specific, write things that happened that day, simple things that make us thankful." We marched side by side along Lakeshore Boulevard. A parade of cars whizzed past, making conversation difficult.

"Sure . . . it sounds like a good idea," I yelled, a little winded as I tried to keep up with her. "How about I e-mail you my list every morning and you e-mail me yours?"

Karen and I have set other challenges for each other in the past. *Save money. Pray more. Lose weight. Give back. Drink less wine. Spend less money. Get in shape.* But this was different. I had to be accountable on a daily basis. Which meant I had to be intentional *and* I had to be grateful.

The first day was easy. In my list I included the walk I'd had with Karen, the ten-dollar bill I found in my rain-coat pocket and the ripe avocado I had for my salad. The second day, I forgot about being grateful until I was getting ready for bed. It wasn't a good workday for me. No matter how long I sat and wrote, I felt like a miner digging for gold in a depleted mine. As I scrubbed my cheeks with my gentle face cleanser, I thought, *Crap . . . what five things do I have to be grateful for today? I didn't do the dishes, didn't file that mound of bills I have been promising to clean up for a month, and instead of walking the dog, I took a nap. I was a lump in front of the computer all day, and everything I wrote was crap, crap, crap—how am I going to come up with five things to be thankful for?*

I pounded back downstairs to make sure once again the house was locked tight as Fort Knox, an obsessive routine I developed after both my sons left for college. French doors—check. Windows—check. As I walked past the powder room, I was horrified to see a candle still lit. The door had been closed tight, and the candle-light made the room all toasty and warm, bathing it in an amber glow—a glow that could have ignited the wall-paper while I slept. I blew it out and doused it with cold water. With the tap running full blast, I prayed. *Thank you, God, for letting me see this candle—thank you for protecting me.* My heart hammered as I hurried from room to room to make sure the other candles had been snuffed.

Tucked safe in my bed, I thought about how lucky I was, about what might have happened if I hadn't rechecked the house. I punched my pillow, surprised I was sleepy even though I'd snuck in that delicious nap on the couch. My hulking black Lab approached me for his good night pat on the head. "Sorry I didn't walk you today, buddy. Tomorrow will be better." He nudged my hand with his heavy head. I dug my fingers deep into his thick black coat and massaged his neck. When he'd had enough, he headed for his bed. He scratched and stomped on his mattress until he found the most comfy spot, where he plopped down with a thud and moaned. Before I fell asleep, I wrote my list in my head.

Five things I am grateful for today:

1. *afternoon naps*
2. *obsessive routines*
3. *God's protection*
4. *a dog who loves me even when I don't walk him*
5. *listing five grateful things*

P.S. Today I am mostly grateful for you, Deb. For your courage, your amazing spirit, and your belief in miracles.

Let us be thankful.

—Hebrews 12:28

Candle Love

Dear Deb,

Michael turned four a few months before Patrick's first birthday. Together we made a small round chocolate cake for his baby brother. We iced it with dark chocolate frosting made with Godiva cocoa and butter, and Michael decorated it with rainbow-colored sprinkles and tiny M & M's. As we sang "Happy Birthday" to Patrick, he sat in his high chair, waving his arms up and down like he was conducting a symphony. His chestnut eyes shone bright with the light from the single candle in front of him. He blew it out, dug his fist deep into the cake, grabbed a handful of gooey chocolate, and filled his mouth with joy.

The next day, Michael woke earlier than normal. The late January morning was still black as night as I sat at the kitchen table, reading the paper and sipping my mug of Irish breakfast tea. "Mommy, I'm sad," Michael said as he scooted up onto my lap. I had just finished my bran flakes. Michael dipped his finger into the leftover milk in my bowl and licked it clean. "Did you have a bad dream, honey?" I asked. I felt his forehead for fever in case he confused feeling sad with feeling sick.

"No, I didn't dream, Mommy. I'm sad because I think now that Patrick is here you might run out of love." He sobbed and buried his face in my chest. I combed his silky curls with my fingers and started to rock him back and forth, something that calmed both of us since he had gone through his tantrum stage.

"I will never run out of love, honey. I have enough love for both you and Patrick." I kissed the top of his head. It smelled like fresh-picked apples.

He looked up at me with tearstained cheeks and watery eyes. "How do you know you have enough love?"

"Wait here." I sat him in the chair next to me where he could watch me while I grabbed four tall, white, tapered candles from the dining room buffet. I placed them in front of Michael one by one. "This candle here is me." I pointed to the first one. "This one is Daddy, this one is you, and the last one is Patrick." I lined them up in front of him, a family of candles sitting on shiny brass feet. I lit my candle first. "The flame on my candle is my love, honey. Watch what happens when I share it with Daddy." I lit his dad's candle using mine. Michael's eyes widened as he stared at the two flames flickering in concert close to his face. I continued to light the other two candles using the mommy candle until all four candles danced with light. "Is the flame on my candle going out?" I asked.

Michael got up on his knees to examine the flame. He tilted his head to the left and to the right as he stared at the bright yellow glow. "No, Mommy, your fire can't go out," he said. "It's way too shiny."

"I will turn the darkness into light."

—Isaiah 42:16

Perfectly Imperfect

Dear Deb,

"Come look, Margie dear!" Grandma called in her Scottish brogue that rolled thick as porridge off her tongue. She lowered herself in the middle of the abandoned road. "Kneel doon here a'side me for a wee bit." She patted a spot on the cracked pavement next to her. A breeze caught the brim of her white floppy hat, and it smacked against her forehead. My favorite walk with Grandma was on this old stretch of crooked road that used to be the Kings Highway 69. On one side a wall of bedrock loomed high above us, and on the other side a small lake buzzed with swamp life. Dragonflies with gossamer wings and luminous emerald heads flitted above water lilies, in search of lunch bugs. Some were hooked together in pairs. Dozens of creamy-white lilies were in full bloom, their open blossoms like teacups floating on lush green saucers.

"Did you know that a wee ant can carry twenty-five times its own weight?" Grandma asked. "Isn't that just a marvelous thing?" A single line of ants marked a trail inches away from her sensible lace-up walking shoes. "That would be the same as you trying to carry a refrigerator. Do you think you could do that, Margie?" One of the ants dropped an amber seed twice his size. He circled round, picked it up again, and continued to follow the others.

"Will all these ants make it across the road?" I turned toward the pond to see if I could discover where they started.

"They won't give up until they get to their nest. They live in colonies, dear, ant villages, and they all help each other." Grandma grunted as she pushed herself up. *"Och aye . . ."* She sighed. "So many amazing wee things in God's big world."

I walked over to the edge of the pond and pitched a fist-sized chunk of slate into the pond. I jumped back when the splash almost reached my face.

"The Queen's Lace is in bloom!" Grandma stood on the shoulder of the road amid a cluster of lacey white flowers that were almost as tall as her. My dad joked everyone was taller than Grandma. I was a foot shorter than her, but no matter how tall I grew, I knew she still would be bigger than me. "Come, Margie. Let's pick some to take home."

There were hundreds of them, a ballet of delicate lacey blooms swaying back and forth on erect mossy green stems thin as strands of spaghetti. "Some people call this a weed—how daft." She stretched her arms wide and let her hands hover over the tops of the blooms. "These are wildflowers, not weeds. And they're named for Anne, a strong, beautiful queen who loved to make lace."

I drew a blossom towards my face—it smelled like salad! I was surprised until I noticed the feathery leaves on the stem looked like the parsley growing in Grandma's garden.

"They may look fragile, but believe me, dear, they can grow anywhere. In a thicket of thorns, in a rock bed, a farmer's field." Grandma squinted and scanned the road ahead. "In God's world, you don't have to look strong to be strong." She removed her thick glasses and untucked her yellow blouse to polish them with her shirttail. "Och aye, you know that, wee Margie, don't you, hen?" She eyed me. "Just because you don't come from a tended garden, you should never let anyone call you a weed."

"What's that dot in the middle, Grandma?" A tiny speck of blackish red poked out of the center of each lacey bloom.

"Oh, now, that's a story, dear." Grandma pinched the stem of one of the blossoms with her fingernails until it snapped off. "One day Queen Anne pricked herself with her needle while she was making her beloved lace, and her blood stained the piece she was working on." Grandma handed the flower to me and smiled. "That dot reminds us how much beauty there can be in imperfection."

Perfect in beauty, God shines forth.
—Psalm 50:2

Coffee and the Minister

Dear Deb,

I had finally agreed to have that coffee with Ruth, the associate pastor from my new church.

The little café we chose was full. Mothers sipped lattes as they balanced toddlers on their knees. A few business types gulped their dark roasts while answering e-mails on their laptops. I sat at a table for two in front of a crackling fire that was so hot I felt my cheeks flush. My café chair bobbed from side to side on the uneven flagstone floor each time I shifted my weight.

Ruth asked me a few easy questions about my childhood, where I was from, and my church history. She explained one of the best parts of her job was to get to know new people at her church, even new ones like me who hadn't been to church in over twenty-five years.

Something about having coffee alone with a minister makes your secrets bolt from their hiding place. I confused coffee with confession and told Ruth everything. I told her about my divorce, and my fantasies about running away. I shared how I wanted to be a nun in high school and how I was drinking too much red wine to help me sleep. And I told her about my mother.

"My mom was twenty-five years old with four of us under six when she had her first shock treatments. My dad would take her to the hospital in the morning and fetch her after work. She had them as an outpatient in 1958, if you can imagine. My job was to keep my sisters quiet when she came home because the treatments made her sleep so much."

Ruth sipped her tea. "That must have been quite a chore for such a little girl. How did you manage to keep them quiet?"

"I told stories." I didn't tell Ruth that we had no books in our house, that I learned to read from the Sears catalog. "We had this big tattered couch that held all four of us. We'd huddle together and I would make things up . . . you know, stories of having superpowers, faraway worlds. I made up whatever it took to keep my sisters quiet."

"I can't imagine how hard that was for you, Margaret. You must have had a challenging childhood, if you had one at all," Ruth whispered as she reached over to place her hand over mine.

Her touch brought me back to reality. I was mortified I had told Ruth so much. This Caribou Coffee was my hangout, a place where Vivaldi strained to be heard on ancient speakers, a place where chatter bounced off the vaulted ceiling like an echo. Not a place for confession.

I barely knew Ruth, and here I was, telling her way too many secrets. I slid my hand off the table and excused myself to go to the bathroom. When I returned, Ruth had cleaned our table and was writing something in a small spiral-bound journal. I sat back down on my teeter-totter chair and decided I wasn't going to answer any more questions. I turned around to slip my jacket off the back of my chair when Ruth stopped me.

"I want to pray for you, Margaret." She reached across the table to clasp my hand and closed her eyes before I could exclaim, "Pray?"

Here? At our table?

In the daylight? At my hangout?

Ruth prayed in a hushed but very purposeful voice that sounded like Anne Bancroft.

"Dear Lord, thank you for Margaret."

I thought of Dustin Hoffmann in *The Graduate*, "Mrs. Robinson, are you trying to seduce me?"

I bowed my head a teeny bit because I thought if both of us had our heads down, people might think we were reading the graffiti on our table or that we were concentrating on a serious problem, like how to end world hunger. My eyes never stopped darting left, right, in front, to see if anyone I might know was watching.

She continued, "I feel so blessed you have brought Margaret into my life and that she has graced me with some of her stories. You already know about her child-hood and her poor sick mother, Lord, and you know she is hurting right now. She is feeling that life is impossible with a divorce breaking her heart, so I ask you to help her,

Lord. Help Margaret see that everything will work out and that anything is possible with you."

Tears threatened my mascara, and I wasn't sure which was worse, crying or praying in public. I wanted to cover my face with my hands or crawl under the tiny table for two. I peeked down at the floor and saw muffin crumbs, a stained napkin, and a pacifier with a pink handle. I considered sticking the pacifier in my mouth.

After that first coffee, I continued to attend Ruth's church. For some reason, it reminded me of coming home after a long vacation, when you breathe in your own house smells, and you stop for a moment to say, "Boy, it's good to be home."

I didn't see Ruth every Sunday, but she called me each week to give me the same message, whether I answered the phone or not.

"Hello, dear Margaret. I am thinking about you and want you to know that I love you and that God loves you more." She would emphasize *love*, drawing it out like Elvis Presley singing "Love Me Tender," which always made me smile.

P.S. I love you, Deb. And God loves you more.

We love because he first loved us.
—1 John 4:19

Motown Magic

Dear Deb,

When he was in the tenth grade, Michael enlisted my help with a music project. Each student was charged with interviewing parents for a list of fifteen of their favorite songs of all time. The class was going to compare lists and graph a time line based on the year the parents were born. Michael reminded me my whole list couldn't be Motown, something he thought would be embarrassing.

I had five days to complete this task. I loved that I was being asked to contribute to a school project! The years of being room mom and volunteering in the classroom ended once Michael entered middle school. It was a big adjustment from being the "cool" mom who brought cookies for the whole class to being the mom he pretended he didn't know whenever his friends were around.

For five days I never stopped listening to music. I cleaned the house to Motown, cooked to classical music and read at night to movie soundtracks and opera. After three days, I had narrowed my list down to one hundred songs. How was I ever going to choose fifteen favorites when I had so many? It was harder than choosing my favorite food. Goat cheese. No, wait. French fries. No, chocolate!

Two weeks after Michael handed in my list, he mentioned in passing that I wasn't the only parent who listed more than one Motown song. He never mentioned it again, and I forgot about the project with the hustle and bustle of Thanksgiving and Christmas approaching.

On Christmas morning Michael waited until all the gifts had been opened before he handed me a small box neatly wrapped with gold foil paper. I opened it, commenting on the beautiful wrapping and how much I loved gold paper. When I lifted the lid from the box, I gasped. Sitting like a precious silver egg in a nest of white tissue paper was a single CD. In black marker Michael had written *Mom's Favorites.*

That was ten years ago, and I still sigh each time I remember how Michael orchestrated his gift of love. Anytime I hear one of those fifteen songs and Michael is with me, we look at each other and smile.

I will sing and make music with all my soul.
—Psalm 108:1

P.S. *Mom's Favorites* are listed below, the CD a little worse for wear, but working!

"Ain't No Mountain High Enough"
"Old Time Rock 'n' Roll"
"Pachelbel's Canon in D"
"Time to Say Goodbye"
"Vivaldi's The Four Seasons"
"Amazing Grace"
"Heard It Through the Grapevine"
"When a Man Loves a Woman"
"What a Wonderful World"
"There's a Place for Us"
"Billie Jean"
"Pavorotti's Nessun Dorma"
"My Girl"
"You're the First, the Last, My Everything"
"People"

Fabulous

Dear Deb,

"I have always wanted one of these!" Lisa exclaimed. She hugged the generous collar of the lush, white terry robe and strolled past me like a runway model. It was hard to believe my baby sister was fourteen years old, harder to believe I had just turned thirty-two. Lisa was the only one of five sisters to get the tall gene. With her height and lean build, she could have graced the cover of *Seventeen* magazine. Her complexion was milky and dusted with cinnamon freckles that danced across her nose. But it was her watchful russet eyes on a mission for approval that would have appealed to every teenage girl flipping through the magazine pages in search of a better self.

"I *need* one . . . I need a robe like this to wear after I have a shower. Can I take this home too?" Lisa flopped on the bed beside her stash of treasures. Two discs of lavender French-milled soaps wrapped in yellow tissue and numerous tiny bottles filled with luxurious creams and bath oil. Like the robe she was wearing, everything was monogrammed with the golden lion seal of the Ritz Carlton Hotel, Montreal.

"Sorry, honey. You can't take the robe home. Robes aren't a freebie. You can wear it as much as you want, but it stays at the hotel."

Lisa jumped up and headed to the bathroom to search for more hotel riches. Her excitement made me weary. I had lost my enthusiasm for five-star hotels after too many days in conference rooms filled with strangers and too many lonely nights with room service. No matter how exciting the city, I was returning home to the same empty apartment every week. It had been eighteen months since I'd left Greece and my home at sea on board the *Stella Solaris*. I had spent a glorious year sailing the Mediterranean with stops in the Greek Islands, Egypt, and Israel, places I had only dreamed of one day seeing. Once I was stationed back home in Canada as their sales manager, I was excited to send others to the most beautiful places in the world, but after two years of knocking on travel agents' doors, my cruise director smile was looking more tired than my luggage.

Montreal was the start of another four-week sales marathon that involved seminars in a dozen cities. Instead of flying from city to city, I coordinated a road trip throughout eastern Canada and invited Lisa to spend her summer with me. She jumped at the chance. To her, I was living a fabulous life selling luxury cruises to the rich and famous. She had no idea how lonely I was. No one did. Not even my family knew that what I really wanted was to meet Mr. Right and make Mr. and Mrs. Right babies. At thirty-two, I feared I might be alone the rest of my life.

When Marc approached me in Montreal, I couldn't believe he picked me, with all the other beautiful women in the room. With his mahogany tan, navy sports jacket, and crisp white shirt, he looked like he should have been sipping scotch at the yacht club instead of attending a hotel breakfast seminar for one hundred travel agents. I accepted his dinner invitation when he included Lisa.

"What was it like working and living on a cruise ship?" Marc sat sardined between Lisa and me at a tiny bistro table big enough for two.

"Oh . . . living on a ship was so *incredible*." I let *incredible* hang in the air, hoping he would think I was. "I mean, the Mediterranean was *fabulous*. I would wake up one day in Turkey, the next day in Egypt . . . and Santorini is *so* amazing—you can touch heaven there." I sipped my red wine, careful not to let any dribble down my chin. "It was a floating five-star hotel, and since I was in charge of the captain's table, I met some of the most *fabulous* people . . . a Supreme Court judge from the States, a countess from Denmark, and a few celebrities." Marc didn't ask which celebrities (something everyone asked), so I kept going, certain I would say something to impress him. "I've been to Jerusalem six times, but it got a little old, so I eventually grabbed a limo to Tel Aviv when I had time off and hung out there."

Lisa coughed and looked up at the ceiling. A blue haze

hovered above our heads. We were one of the few tables without a smoker. Marc asked me a question about Cairo, but after that he was silent. When he started glancing at his watch, I kept talking to fill in the silence. I was sure I could dazzle him with my adventures in the Turkish bath in Istanbul or impress him with the storm that almost capsized the *Stella Solaris* on the French coast.

By the time I finished my crème caramel, I realized Marc wasn't the only one who was quiet. Lisa hadn't uttered a word during the whole dinner. After a brisk good-bye, he hailed a cab in front of the restaurant, and Lisa and I decided to walk back to the Ritz Carlton. It was a perfect summer night, the balmy breeze a seductive blanket beckoning a sleepover under the stars.

"What did you think of Marc?" I asked. I sniffed the palm of my hand, hoping it would carry his woodsy scent from our farewell handshake.

Lisa had stopped in front of a shoe shop with a window dressed like a birthday party. Ribbons of streamers hung from the ceiling like glittery rain. They puddled around leather sandals more colorful than a bowl of tropical fruit jelly beans.

"He was OK," Lisa muttered. "But *you* were weird."

"What do you mean I was weird?" I worried that I had started speaking a little French or Greek while I was flirting with Marc, something I had done without realizing it since returning to Canada.

"You were so *phony!*" Lisa exclaimed. "I hardly recognized you. All you talked about was how *fa-a-abulous* your life is, how much you have traveled, and how many important people you know." She hurled the words like stones, each one heavier than the last. I wanted to put my hands over my face.

"You never let Marc talk. All you did was blah-blah this and blah-blah that!" Lisa stomped her foot. "No wonder you don't have a boyfriend!"

I stared at her, dumbstruck. I was not *phony*. I *did* go to all those places. I *was* being me at dinner. I was being the best me I knew how to be. Didn't I have a *fabulous* job? Why should Marc need to know any more about me than that? I turned and walked away from Lisa, afraid that if I spoke I would lash out and ruin the start of our adventure.

"Margie, why can't you just be you?" she called after me. "Just be you, and everyone will love you the way I do."

Lisa was right. For years I had been acting like I had a perfect life and didn't need anyone. I knew it prevented people from getting too close to me. But knowing it wasn't enough to make me stop doing it. I had been seeking comfort in the land of *fa-a-a-abulous* my whole life. No matter how tiring it was to act like life was so great, I never gave up the hope that if I kept pretending it was, it eventually would be. I was afraid if I gave any voice to the heart that Lisa loved, it would sing the truth of my childhood and I would never be the same.

Lisa caught up to me and nudged my shoulder. When I looked into her watchful eyes, I wanted to wrap my arms around her and tell her I loved her for being so brave and honest, to tell her she was right. But my arms were sentries posted at my sides, and the words strained my jaw like a wad of gum too big to chew.

"Hey," I said, "why don't we find a café that's open and get some chocolate croissants?" I scanned the street, locked arms with her, and skipped toward the Ritz Carlton Hotel.

> *"People look at the outward appearance,*
> *but the Lord looks at the heart."*
>
> —1 Samuel 16:7

Delightful

Dear Deb,

I wasn't sure what was worse about moving in May—
starting at a new school with only seven weeks left before
summer vacation or Dad moving out again.

It was a long walk from our new apartment to Sacred
Heart School, and even though I did a dress rehearsal twice,
we were late our first day. My sisters and I had to wait in the
hallway in front of the principal's office, where we watched
the parade of students marching past in no hurry to get to
their classrooms. I looked down at my scuffed white sneakers and immediately wished I hadn't. A burr had hitched a
ride on my shoelace, and the tangled mess was pasted to
my ankle sock. I wanted to peel off my socks and throw
them in the trash before I met my new teacher. But Mom
said only Protestants wore shoes without socks.

When Sister Ignatius escorted me to my fourth grade
class, Mr. Lees was pointing his yardstick at the map of

Europe that hung in front of the blackboard. He smiled when he saw me. "Thank you, Sister," he said. I thought maybe I should thank her too, especially since we were late, but when I turned around, she had vanished in a big cloud of black.

Mr. Lees shepherded me to the front row. He placed his hands on my shoulders. "Class, this is Margaret Malcolmson. She just moved here from St. John's School. I hear she got 100% in Spelling."

Someone belched in the back of the room, and a pretty girl with a purple headband and a long thick pony-tail whipped around to face him. "Robert, you are a P-I-G." She flicked her ponytail with the back of her hand, then reached down to adjust her ankle sock. That's when I noticed her shoes. Black patent T-straps with inch-high heels. Real Princess Anne heels. I wanted to be her friend right away.

"And in case you are interested, *your* final spelling exam is in three weeks." Mr. Lees motioned to the empty desk in front of me. The front row! My favorite place to sit. I loved the front row because I hated missing anything the teacher said. But as soon as I sat at the desk, I knew Mr. Lees had made a mistake to sit me there. Two brand-new fat pencils lay in the pencil well, their shiny lead tips sharp as a darning needle. A new pink eraser, full inkwell, and two composition notebooks sat stacked in the center of the desk. I wanted to open the composition book to breathe in the scent of new paper, a cleaner smell than laundry dried on the line. But I didn't touch a thing. They had to belong to someone else.

The recess bell rang, and thirty-five kids lined up against the blackboard, frisky colts waiting to race to freedom. I stayed at my desk.

When the room had emptied, Mr. Lees stood beside me. "Is there something wrong, Margaret?" His kind eyes were the same khaki color as his rumpled dress pants. The hems were frayed and dark where they dragged on the floor.

"Are you sure this is my desk?" I asked. "These supplies must belong to someone else—everything is all new."

"Those are for you, Margaret. I wanted to get you a welcome present to let you know how glad I am to have you in my class. I called your teacher at St. John's to get some information about you, and she told me how much you liked to write stories." He walked away and started brushing the blackboard. "That's your desk, and those are your supplies if you want them."

If I want them? Two brand-new composition books for my stories, new sharpened pencils, and an eraser with clean ends!

"Oh, and by the way . . ." He smacked the brush against his leg like he was putting out a fire. "Your teacher also told me you were a delight to have in her class and that I was lucky to have you in mine."

That night I wrote my first entry in my new composition book. I wrote: *A delight. Mr. Lees says I am.* I wrote it on the very last page so I'd have something to look forward to after I'd filled it with my stories. I promised myself I wouldn't turn to that last page even if we moved again. And I didn't because a funny thing happened every time I opened that notebook. No matter what page I was on, I could hear Mr. Lees. *You are a delight.*

A word aptly spoken is like apples
of gold in settings of silver.
—Proverbs 25:11

It's a Miracle!

Dear Deb,

Ever since I can remember, I have loved magic. As a little girl, I ooohed and ahhhed the loudest when a magician would dig deep into his top hat and pull out miles of vibrant silk scarves. How did he fit so many scarves in his tall black hat? How did he tie all those knots with me watching him so closely? I loved the mystery of it all!

Over the years I've learned to catch the sleight of hand when a magician palms a red spongy ball, and more than once I've caught him slipping the gold coin into his heavily starched cuff. It feeds my ego to catch the trick, but it also makes me sad to lose the mystery that delighted me as a young girl.

Thank God for miracles! Miracles are unexplainable, and no one can ever catch their trick—miracles seem natural, yet they contradict nature as we know it. Maybe that's why so many people have a hard time believing what they see and instead choose doubt over awe. Not me. I've seen an eagle with his beady amber eyes soar a hundred feet above a spring-fed lake and swoop down to catch a pickerel mini ding his own business a foot under the surface of the darkest waters. I've seen tiny crocus buds with lavender petals soft as a baby's eyelash birth their way through wet, crusty snow. Miracles both.

Perhaps miracles are supposed to tickle the child in us to remind us that mystery is magic. What greater mystery than making a blind man see? Or feeding five thousand hungry people with only five loaves of bread? Today when I read the stories of Jesus' miracles, I don't ask how he did it, and I don't search for a logical explanation like I did with those illusion makers of my childhood. My faith tells me Jesus did it because he is God. Mystery? Yes. But as Einstein said, the most beautiful thing we can experience is the mysterious.

Miracles are also one of God's ways of getting our attention. I know he got mine. It's a miracle I'm here.

Two people have tried to kill me. The first person was my mother. When she discovered at eighteen years old she was pregnant with me, the shame for a good Catholic girl was crushing. She felt her only option was to throw herself down a flight of concrete stairs to kill the baby. Mom was battered and bruised, but my teeny heart continued to beat. The second person who tried to end my life was me. Twenty-seven years later, I was in the same situation as Mom. Different circumstances, but still felt like I was out of options. On a rainy Sunday night, I made a plan to drive my car off a mountain pass. I pushed the accelerator to the floor and sped down the pass until I reached the opening where I'd decided to steer my little Volkswagen through the guardrail into the black void. When I tried to turn the wheel, I couldn't. The steering wheel had locked. I yanked it with both arms and every bit of strength I had, but it wouldn't budge. I don't remember how, but my little car managed to steer itself home.

Miracle. The word conjures up images of being healed, of being saved. Miracle. Gifts from heaven made in heaven. I used to believe there were big miracles and little miracles. But I'm not so sure God measures miracles. Whether helping a blind man see or designing eagle eyes, I think every miracle is God talking to us. *Open your eyes. See this. Here I am.* Thirty years ago on a dark rainy night when life made me feel I had no options, a miracle showed me I did.

Oh, Deb! How blessed we are that miracles are sprinkled everywhere. Thank you for asking me to believe in yours.

> *"He performs wonders that cannot be*
> *fathomed, miracles that cannot be counted."*
> —Job 5:9

God Shows Up

Dear Deb,

Late afternoon on Christmas Eve, I walked around the house from room to room like a mama dog who forgets her puppies have been adopted. Michael and Patrick were spending their first Christmas with their dad. Everyone I knew in Minnesota was dressed in their Sunday best, sharing traditions with their families and singing "Joy to the World" like they meant it. I was still wearing my pink flannel pj's with the martini-drinking kittens. Flannel pajamas had been my uniform for months.

I wandered to the kitchen to start the teakettle and saw my poor cat in a tangled mess on the hardwood floor. Mittens had knocked down one of the Christmas cards taped to the basement door. She was in a frenzy trying to shake off a small card stuck to her forepaw, and the more she shook, the more the tape tangled and matted her fur. I sat on the floor, murmuring sweet nothings until she stopped flailing, and I helped peel away the tape and card.

The card was from my pastor, Ruth. I had received it in the mail that morning mixed in with the piles of Christmas greetings from the trash removal service and the gas, phone, and electric companies. All of them wished me a joyous season and successful New Year even though I owed them money. Ruth's card stood out because it was so simple. It was smaller than the other cards and all white except for a two-inch detailed etching of a tiny baby in a manger. Below the etching the word *love* was written in script so fine it looked like a whisper.

The card was blank inside except for Ruth's hand-written message. Her petite penmanship with tiny, teacher-perfect letters looked like rows of forget-me-nots.

> *Merry Christmas, Margaret.*
> *My gift to you is Luke 1:37.*
> *Love, Ruth*

I had no idea what Luke 1:37 was, but laughed at her blatant attempt to get me to read the Bible again. She had snuck one into my mailbox that fall and wedged it sideways on top of the bills and free offers for a cleaner furnace and a firmer me. Her yellow sticky note on the cover said, "Read me 15 minutes a day." It reminded me of Alice in Wonderland's note, *Drink Me*, and I wondered what would happen if I read it.

How was I supposed to read the Bible when I couldn't concentrate long enough to read how to microwave a frozen pizza? Breathing would have been impossible if I had to concentrate to do it. Mittens leaned against me and purred as I slid my hand down her back and watched the tufts of loose fur float behind her tail.

I opened Ruth's card again. *My gift to you is Luke 1:37.* I wanted to call her to ask what the heck Luke 1:37 was, but she had gone to work at a mission in Paraguay for the holidays. I closed her card and taped it back on the basement door where I had been taping cards every Christmas for the last fifteen years. This year, all the cards just ticked me off. Cheery Santas and family photos of happy couples with their coiffed children and Labrador retrievers looked as fake as a cheap toupee.

I wished that Ruth were in town. I needed her to remind me of that promise she gave me about God helping me get through my divorce. I needed to hear her say, "I love you, Margaret, and God loves you more," because as I stared at those cards taped to my basement door, I realized that for the first time I my life, I didn't know what to do. I felt like I might disintegrate like toilet paper. One flush and I'd be gone. I changed my mind about the tea and hurried to get dressed for a walk. I was hoping the frigid Minnesota temperatures would numb my pain.

Fresh snow covered my front lawn like a fur blanket. The only blemishes were playful rabbit tracks crisscrossing each other. Even the blacktop on the newly plowed roads was white, the frozen ground prevailing against the sun.

Within twenty minutes, I realized I had underestimated the biting cold, which was probably why there was no one else walking around. My toes tingled as if they had gone to sleep, and my fingertips felt like I had dipped them in scalding water. I needed to find a place to get warm.

I was glad a few boutiques along Lake Street were still open for last-minute shopping. I slipped into a shop in a renovated bungalow called the Hunt Queens. An overhead bell chimed, announcing my arrival as I walked into Christmas Wonderland. Tiny white fairy lights twinkled everywhere like a Christmas forest filled with fireflies; shortbreads shaped like hearts and angels were presented on cut-glass platters; and a massive silver tray was piled high with a mountain of chocolate-dipped strawberries. The scent of fresh-cut juniper, cinnamon, and apples made me yearn for my grandma, who had died seven years earlier. Christmas abundance covered every surface in the store. Sterling bowls heaped with pomegranates and mandarin oranges reminded me of the Christmas party we used to have every year for our neighbors. Back when I had a life.

A stunning blonde woman dressed in a winter white wool pantsuit was humming "O Come All Ye Faithful" along with the Mormon Tabernacle Choir. Her rich scarlet lipstick was a stark contrast to her white suit. "Merry Christmas!" she exclaimed. "Were you out walking in this?" Her hand flew to her face, and I noticed her manicured nails painted the same scarlet red.

I looked like a refugee from Siberia. In my hurry to get out of the house, I had grabbed Michael's woolen ski cap and pulled it down past my eyebrows. I had wrapped a red tartan scarf around my face to protect my mouth and nose. And I was wearing sunglasses that were dark enough to alert the paparazzi.

"I heard it's almost thirty below with the windchill," she continued as I peeled my scarf from my face. I wondered if she'd think I was a boy with my hair tucked into Michael's hat and his down ski jacket gobbling up my 5'3" frame. I hated looking so crappy at Christmas. I wanted to look as lovely as she did. I wanted to be wearing makeup, a designer suit, and killer heels.

"Oh, I just felt like going for a walk with all the activity at my house. My kids are busy wrapping presents while their friends are playing Nintendo, if you can imagine that on Christmas Eve." A big fat lie. The same as the ones I told everyone about how happy we were. I glanced at her wedding ring with a diamond the size of a school bus and knew she had a husband and children at home, which was the only thing I wanted.

She walked over to a small table and offered me some hot cider, which I gratefully took to warm my fingers. I noticed her merchandise, a combination of old and new, and I felt like I could have been in my own living room. Vintage floral oil paintings, antique crystal chandeliers, and mirrors in gilt frames looked so similar to my own.

"Have you been in the store before?" she asked.

"No, but I've heard about it. I collect antiques and love things that tell a story. I don't need anything in particular though." I headed towards a blue painted cabinet filled with creamy linens and fought the urge to ask if she had any husbands for sale in the back room who meant "forever" when they said it.

"Hey," she exclaimed, "if you like things with a story, you might like this painting I just put out this morning."

Couldn't she tell from how I looked that I wasn't in

there to shop? That what I needed I couldn't buy? She turned and reached behind her to remove it from the wall. She held it in both hands to appraise it. "It's an old watercolor, no date, but reminds me of one of those 'Home Sweet Home' paintings . . . you know, nostalgic like that." She stretched out her arms to examine it at a distance. "Except I've never seen this in a painting before . . . Do you know anything about the Bible?"

I stopped sipping my cider and tried to look, but she stepped away to grab a dustcloth. She laid the painting on the counter. "It's a piece of Scripture, and it's pretty accurate because I called my business partner this morning and asked her to look it up in her Bible." She smiled. "I wasn't familiar with it, but maybe you are. My partner said it's Luke 1:37." She wiped the glass.

I put my cup down and held my breath. I pictured Mittens, the tape, my card from Ruth.

"Did you say *Luke 1:37*?" I unzipped my jacket and fanned my face with my scarf. I sounded like I had laryngitis.

"Yeah, that's what the painting is." She flipped it up to show me. "See?"

I reached out and touched the glass. It was an old watercolor with a soft creamy background stained in a few spots where someone might have spilled tea. About thirty inches wide and ten inches tall, the painting was surrounded by a half-inch wooden frame painted white, chipped and worn on the edges. In one corner, the artist had painted a small wooden bridge arching from a rocky island to the mainland where a few lonely pine trees guarded the shore. The main body of the painting was a tranquil blue sea, and if you looked closely to where the sea met the horizon, the artist had painted three vertical black lines, a half-inch tall. They were masts of sailboats miles from shore, deadlocked in a windless sea.

The hot cider was starting to make me feel sleepy, and the pine scent that filled the store was stinging my nostrils. I stared at the painting, unbelieving, but believing at the same time. I felt dizzy and confused, the same as I felt the time a magician pulled the entire queen of clubs out of his wallet after I had signed it and ripped it into tiny pieces.

She was right to compare the painting to a Home, Sweet Home needlepoint because what stood out the most was the verse. Above that calm sea, in four-inch Gothic letters, the artist had painted:

With God Nothing Shall Be Impossible.

I took it out of her hands. I needed to feel its weight to make sure it was real. I barely heard her as she continued, "It's pretty rustic, and I almost kept it myself because I kind of like the message, but for some reason, I thought I should just put it out this morning . . ."

I bought it and carried it home.

After searching for an hour, I found the Bible from Ruth at the bottom of a laundry basket. I looked up Luke 1:37 myself, just to be sure. But as I flipped the pages, I knew it would be there exactly like the painting, and when I found it, I caressed the words and read them over and over.

With God nothing shall be impossible.
—Luke 1:37 KJV

The Changed Cross

Dear Deb,

In a very old poem called "The Changed Cross," a woman is feeling overburdened by her life. She feels cheated, is certain her cross is heavier than that of anyone she knows. So she prays and asks God if she can choose a different cross. God says OK because that's the way he is. He leads her to a room filled with crosses of all different shapes, sizes, and colors. Some are mounted on the wall, some leaning against each other, and some piled in hilly mounds on the floor.

The woman is ecstatic; she is thrilled to be able to pick her own cross, one better suited to her strength and abilities. The first one to catch her eye looks as though it belongs to royalty. Smaller than most, it is made of gold and set with rubies, opals, and diamonds. But when she picks it up, she almost falls over backwards with the weight of it. She finds another cross that looks like it was knit with fresh flowers. She tries to find a spot to lift it without damaging any of the fragrant blossoms, and when she discovers a small opening, she wraps her hands around it to test its weight. Piercing thorns beneath the blooms bite into her flesh, and she gasps at the shock of it.

The woman goes from cross to cross trying as many as she can and rejects them all until she finds a simple wooden one. It's almost as tall as she is, and the wood is polished and smooth where it had been carried. It has no embellishments except for a few words inscribed near the base. The woman picks it up and finds it the easiest to carry. Still heavy, but manageable. She feels as though her small hands were made to hold it. When she crouches down to read the inscription, she sees her name on it with a love note: *My child, this is your cross, the one you have carried all along, the one that became too heavy when you tried to carry it alone.**

P.S. Am praying that God lessens the weight of your cross with these new treatments, Deb.

Carrying his own cross, he went out.
—John 19:17

---

*   From L. B. Cowan, *Streams in the Desert*, August 29, http://www.crosswalk.com/devotionals/desert/streams-in-the-desert-aug-29-1418672.html.

Heart Star

Dear Deb,

Patrick was three years old, nestled on my lap for a story, when he looked up at me and asked, "Mama, how much do you love me?"

"With my whole heart," I answered. His strawberry blond curls, soft as a spring dandelion, caressed my neck.

"What does your heart look like?" He laid his hand on my chest and tapped his fingers.

Patrick thought in pictures, but I was sure comparing my heart to something from the butcher shop wasn't what he wanted. I kissed the tips of his fingers while I searched my mind for a heart picture.

"My heart looks like a star, honey . . . the brightest star in the sky."

He furrowed his brow. "But stars only shine at night. Does your heart only work at night?"

I explained that just because we can't see stars during

the day doesn't mean they aren't there, that stars always have light. Patrick jumped off my lap and ran to his closet.

"Come inside with me, Mama, and turn out the lights. I want to see your heart shine."

> *For God, who said, "Let light shine out of darkness," made his light shine in our hearts.*
> — 2 Corinthians 4:6

Summer Reading

Dear Deb,

One summer morning, Mom called me at the cabin to ask for a book recommendation. I took the phone outside and leaned against the railing of our deck. Our shoreline was shaded by the lofty pines surrounding the cabin, but I could see Patrick clearly as he snorkeled round the dock, his newest summer activity. His swim trunks painted with tropical fish glowed neon on the surface of the still lake.

"I just finished that last Mary Higgins Clark book you gave me." Mom was chewing gum, half a stick of Wrigley's spearmint like always. A lady never chews a whole stick. I could hear "Be My Baby" in the background. She was watching *Dirty Dancing* again.

"Did you like that one?" I yawned. The previous summer, Mom had spent a month with us at the cabin. I'd given her a list of novels I thought she'd like. I was determined to get her to read something other than the self-help books she read that only frustrated her.

"I liked *Where Are the Children* better. It was more exciting. I *knew* all along she didn't kill her children."

I had also convinced Mom to get a library card, a ticket to help get her out of the house. It had become more difficult each year for her to leave the safety of her television shows.

"What are you reading now, Margie?" she asked. "I finished everything on that list you gave me and need another book."

"Oh . . . I've been reading the same book all summer," I responded. I wanted to tell her what I was reading but hadn't told anyone yet. I especially wasn't sure how to tell my family.

"It's such a beautiful morning here, Mom. Patrick's already out there at the end of the dock, looking for Boss." Boss was a huge, largemouth bass who lived under our dock. Patrick adopted him and became Boss's body-guard. He'd jump into the lake screaming "Cannonball!" any time a fisherman came close to our shoreline.

"Did you say you've been reading the same book all summer? It must be huge."

"The biggest," I answered, still hoping she wouldn't ask. We'd never had a Bible in our house; I grew up think-ing the only people who read the Bible were priests or those weird guys standing on milk crates, who held card-board signs cautioning us about the end of the world.

"You're usually such a fast reader, Margie. How many pages does it have?"

"One thousand seven hundred and two," I said. "I told you it's a big book, Mom." I knew she would never consider reading a book that was this long. She probably wouldn't ask me the title when she heard how many pages it had.

I heard her blow smoke into the phone. I could almost smell it, even a thousand miles away. Mom hadn't changed her brand in years.

"That sounds more like an encyclopedia . . . or a text-book. Is it one of those long historical books covering years and years, like that *Pillars of the Earth* book you tried to get me to read a few years ago? I couldn't get through *that*. It was like reading the Bible, for Pete's sake."

I took a deep breath and told her that in fact I *was* reading the Bible. Ruth had given it to me that fall, and I had brought it to the cabin even though I hadn't opened it all those months at home. I just kept moving it from room to room like it was a decorative vase I wasn't sure where to put.

Mom cracked her gum over and over. It reminded me of my boys popping plastic Bubble Wrap, a trick they loved to do right in my ear. "The Bible?" She groaned. "Why on earth would you read the *Bible*? You've been hibernating since the divorce, and now you want to read a depressing book? What's wrong with you?"

"I'm getting a divorce, Mom. That's what's wrong with me. I thought I'd be married to David forever; you know that." I was surprised I didn't sound defensive. Maybe it was because I had just finished reading the Psalms, and for the first time in my life I was feeling it was all right to be imperfect. King David, who wrote most of them, was far from perfect, and he was a "drama queen" like me. I had just read one where he begs God to "strike all his enemies in the jaw." I had wanted to punch something for months.

"I can't believe I'm reading the Bible either, because it's not something I ever imagined I'd do, Mom . . . ever." I continued, "I don't know why, but it makes me feel like I'm not so alone anymore."

"Well, I don't know how it possibly can. All those lepers and beggars lying by the side of the road. And they kill Jesus in the end. How can that possibly make you feel better?"

I wasn't very good at being honest with Mom. I had grown up learning that my feelings took a backseat to hers, and I'd never really unlearned it. But after months of therapy since the separation, I was feeling courageous. I never gave up hope that Mom might one day be able to understand me, that she would really hear me and see that I had feelings that mattered.

"Mom, did you know that my whole life I've felt that something was missing? No matter where I lived or who I was with, I yearned for this *thing* I couldn't identify. I searched for it with men, hoping I'd somehow find it in love. I looked for it in my work, which is why I was so ambitious all those years. And every time I traveled to a new country, I'd hope it was there waiting for me." My palms were so sweaty I almost dropped the phone. I couldn't believe she hadn't interrupted me yet. "Even after the boys were born, which made me happier than I could have imagined, I still felt there was something else. Like there was some big secret that happy people had, and it made them better than me." I looked at Patrick again, snorkeling alone without a care in the world other than what he might find on the bottom of our spring-fed lake. I felt that familiar heart tug that made my throat tighten and my eyes water each time I watched my sons from a distance. "Something happens to me when I read the Bible, Mom. The world looks a little different since I've been reading stories about Jesus. I mean, I always knew who he was, but reading how he talked to people makes him more real. He was so kind and so smart. I can't believe how smart he was—"

"Puh-leeeze . . ." She took a long drag of her cigarette and spit the smoke out in one big puff. "Don't tell me that you are going to become one of those Jesus freaks. I always thought you had more sense than that. The Bible can't solve your problems, you know."

If she only knew. I was so devastated about the divorce I might have shaved my head bald and taken tambourine lessons if the Hare Krishna had knocked on my door, promising me comfort.

"Oh, Margie," she went on. "Don't go making things worse by getting all confused about religion. You can't let the Bible interfere with being a mother. You have to stop being so selfish about your own feelings and think about Michael and Patrick. You didn't see me getting all crazy about religion when your father and I divorced."

You're right, I thought. *You were crazy long before your divorce.* I took a deep breath and chose not to take the bait and get hooked into a conversation that had no resolution.

Instead I listened to the same speech I'd been hearing for twenty-five years since Mom and Dad had divorced.

"I had to scrape by to keep you and your sisters together. Do you know how many times we had to move? No matter how bad it got, I was a good mother. You girls always had clean clothes and food on the table . . ."

I considered dropping the phone and sticking my fingers in my ears the way my sons did whenever I tried to have the sex talk with them.

"Do your sisters know that you're reading the Bible?" Mom asked.

"The sisters" were the trump card—a majority agreement could often change Mom's opinion. But I hadn't talked to any of my sisters about the Bible yet, so I didn't answer. I just waited and listened to the silence at the other end and wondered why long-distance silence was so loud. A hummingbird buzzed past me, heading for his feeder, his ruby throat brilliant in the midday sun. He was probably on his way next door to my neighbor Jolene's, where she could read her Bible every day without having to defend it to anyone.

I pictured Mom hanging up and pushing speed dial to have a conference call with all four of my sisters. "Your big sister has lost it," she'd say.

How would I ever be able to explain to her that I hadn't *lost* anything? Instead, I had *found* something—something I couldn't see or touch that was changing that part of me that had been forever waiting to be rescued by a knight.

I thought about Ruth and smiled. I wondered what she would say to my mother. Would she give her a Bible?

Would she send her Christmas cards with codes? I was sure of one thing. Ruth would wrap her arms around Mom and love her the same way she had loved me. Poor Mom. She often said she wished she had cancer. She thought if she had cancer, everyone would feel sorry for her because they'd see how her illness ravaged her when it took over her body; they'd witness the debilitating pain that could cause her to want to stop living. But Mom's kind of pain could never be measured or seen on any X-ray. And like cancer, there was no cure.

I noticed Patrick had stopped swimming and was sitting on the end of the dock, dangling his feet in the lake. He had wrapped a fluffy, navy blue beach towel around his waist, mimicking his dad after a shower. His snorkel and goggles were perched on top of his head, and he was talking to himself or Boss.

I told Mom he needed me, which I often did to end our phone calls. I sighed and said good-bye, wishing I could have told her what happened to me a few weeks earlier.

I had picked the Bible up a dozen times that summer, only to put it back down without opening it. I was worried the Bible would be work, like reading Shakespeare. All I could handle was Dr. Seuss's "Today you are you, that is truer than true."

Turned out that reading the Bible was a boost.

Instant Prozac.

It surprised me with its simple wisdom.

Do not wear yourself out to get rich . . . Cast but a glance at riches, and they are gone. —Proverbs 23:4–5.

How many friends had I seen lose their family homes? How many of them were like us and worked harder at building their stock portfolios than they had at building the foundation for their families?

The morning I'd read that verse, Michael shuffled out of the cabin, yawning like a big, old, worried dog. The summer sun was already leaving its mark on him, bleaching the tips of his thick, cropped hair. At thirteen, he was lean and tanned, and towered over me. He was wearing his faded bathing suit, his summer uniform.

"Morning, Mom. Nice day."

He looked out over the lake as he stretched his arms over his head, palms facing the open blue sky.

"What are you readin'?" He smiled as he reached down to grab my mug of tea; he gulped the last few mouthfuls, our morning ritual.

"My Bible . . . some story from Proverbs," I answered. "Do you know what Proverbs is, Michael?" I assumed he couldn't know since I didn't know until that very morning.

He popped my leftover bits of bagel crusts in his mouth and answered me over his shoulder as he headed toward the water. "Yeah, it's the rules for life written about three thousand years ago. Weren't they written by that dude who was some rich king, who was the son of that David guy? You know, Mom. The one who had the slingshot. Yeah, him . . . whatever."

Then, like a startled young buck, he ran the length of the dock and dove into the lake. And at that moment, it hit me. It hit me just how many people must have read these same rules for life written almost three thousand years ago. Rules about drinking too much wine, about paying taxes, about telling lies.

As I sat in my Adirondack chair in July of 2001, holding in my hands this book filled with wisdom and truth, I realized that millions of people had read the same words. Millions and millions. I was struck with a moment of clarity so profound I could hardly breathe. I felt as insignificant as a grain of sand and as unique as a snowflake at the same time.

I watched my firstborn son glide with powerful strokes along the shoreline of our clear, shallow lake.

I heard myself whisper, *"He knew."*

God knew three thousand years ago that we would be the same. That we would want the same things, that we would have the same needs, and that we would need the same wise words. I thought of how many people have consulted these words—to solve differences, to find answers and meaning in their lives. And I thought of how many have found comfort in these words . . . people in trouble, people at war, hurt people, lost people.

People like me.

Could God have known that I would be sitting on my deck in Spooner, Wisconsin, that day, reading his words that were making my heart race? Was he was watching me at that very moment? I leaned my head back against my chair to look up at the morning sky. The leaves from an aged oak with a canopy covering part of my deck rustled, yet I couldn't feel the wind. A loon called its mate with a haunting wail. As the morning sun warmed my face, I sat as still as I possibly could, savoring the moment. I wanted to say something profound, but all that came out was a whisper.

"Hi, God."

And the sun tickled my face with a million tiny fingers dancing across my skin.

"You will seek me and find me when
you seek me with all your heart."

—Jeremiah 29:13

Better Than Gumballs

Dear Deb,

Many years ago, a friend of mine was struggling with a boss who had anger issues. If he wasn't happy with an employee's performance, he'd hurl his coffee mug across a room without caring where it landed, and as he huffed his way back to his office, he'd knock over every empty chair he passed. Then he'd pout for days. No matter how hard my friend worked at helping him try to find other ways to manage his anger, his boss wouldn't change. "He just can't seem to forgive the smallest slight," my friend told me. "And, people who don't have a forgiving heart can't love with their whole heart."

When my friend quit his job, I thought he was nuts. Back then I never cared about my boss's heart. I cared about my paycheck.

But something about his words stayed with me.

A forgiving heart.

Forgiveness is something I've struggled with most of my life. I know the words and have said them often, even though sometimes I've said them to myself while biting down on my blankets so hard my teeth ached.

I forgive you.

Simple words. But no matter how many times I've said them, I've never been really sure what they meant. Did forgiving mean forgetting? Did it make me weak if I forgave you? Did forgiving mean I give you the chance to hurt me again? I was raised to believe forgiveness was a gift I was supposed to give the person who hurt me, yet that felt like giving a bully an ice cream cone after he pushed me down on the playground, and why would I do that?

When David left, I tried to forgive him for Michael's and Patrick's sakes. I knew a forgiving heart would prevent me from becoming bitter and would help me be a better parent when they needed me most. I thought if I prayed for David, I'd automatically get a forgiving heart, the same way a nickel in a gumball machine gets me a gumball. So I prayed. Over and over on those terrible nights when sleep seemed farther away than heaven, I prayed for David. I prayed even more on the nights I felt like a fraud because my wounded heart didn't mean one word I was saying. But my prayers were as empty as the blanks I left on a test I hadn't studied for, and I eventually stopped.

In his book *What's So Amazing About Grace?* Philip Yancey says forgiveness is a gift we give *ourselves*. When I read that once we truly forgive someone for a wrongdoing, the wrongdoing loses its power to hurt us, I was floored. If that was true, I was ready to run around to everyone who ever hurt me and declare, *"I forgive you, I forgive you, I forgive you!"* The problem was, I could *say* it, but I didn't know how to *do* it. My sense of right and wrong kept getting in the way. And I might have been stuck in that limbo where I allowed blame and judgment to reign if I hadn't learned the most important thing of all from Yancey's wisdom: by forgiving someone, we are trusting that God is a better justice maker than we are. That was the part I was missing as I prayed my empty prayers over and over.

Trust.

Trust in the LORD with all your heart and
lean not on your own understanding.
—Proverbs 3:5

The Open Door

Dear Deb,

For the past two years, I've had a standing date with my dad. Every Monday morning he arrives at 8:30 a.m., and we have coffee and toast with jam while we play cards. Cribbage, a game he taught me at our kitchen table when I was a little girl. He wasn't the kind of dad who ever "let" me win, and I turned into the kind of daughter who doesn't let him win even though he turned eighty-one this year. I have thought about letting him win these past few months, though, as I have noticed the effects of age sneak in—sometimes his hands shake so much when he fans out his cards I wonder how he can see what he's holding. But Dad is too smart, and he would figure it out, which would bother him more than the not winning.

This week as he was dealing the cards, he chatted away about *American Idol,* and I realized we never talk about anything serious. Most Mondays, he walks in the door and asks about Michael and Patrick right after he comments on the weather. When he sips his coffee, he might mention a movie he just saw with his girlfriend, Barb, or tell me about the roast chickens on sale at Fortino's. We don't discuss politics, religion, or feelings, and we never ask each other for advice. More than once, I have wished he was the wise, selfless *Father Knows Best* kind of dad or a financial benefactor I could rely on, but he's never been that kind of dad. He was the kind of dad who left a lot when I was young. But now it seems he is here to stay, and after a twenty-year estrangement, he has woven his way into my heart. I've learned much about him from playing cards. Things that define the man he is now, not the man he used to be. Things that define character, and things I will always remember:

* He is always in a good mood.
* I have never heard him say a bad thing about anyone.
* He is never late.
* When I don't feel well, he phones me every day until he knows I feel better.
* He encourages me to keep at it with my memoir even though he's read stories that don't paint him in an ideal light.
* When I apologize for saying something snarky, he says, "Don't worry about it—it's already forgotten."
* His eyes get all misty when I tell me stories about acts of kindness.

People often say that actions speak louder than words. Dad shows up every Monday, rain or shine. And every Monday I'm excited to open the door.

*Dear children, let us not love with words
or speech but with actions and in truth.*

—1 John 3:18

Every Little Thing

Dear Deb,

After the divorce, Patrick couldn't sleep. For months he camped out on the floor beside my bed because he was afraid to be alone. He kept me awake all night asking those impossible questions a ten-year-old asks: "If you had to choose between being blind or deaf, what would you choose? If you could only have one son, would you name him Michael or Patrick?"

I consulted our pediatrician, who said it was time for Patrick to learn how to self soothe, and although I could help him, he had to go back to his own room. We tried hot baths, mugs of cocoa, back massages, and reading for hours. I bought a *Classical Music for Sleep* CD and sang the song tracks from *Oliver* and *Grease*, but nothing I did helped him fall asleep. One night after I finished reading *The Stinky Cheese Man* and sang a few verses of "Where Is Love," I knelt on the floor beside his bed.

"Patrick, I was thinking we should pray tonight. We could ask God to help you fall asleep and stay asleep. What do you think?" I was stepping outside my comfort zone, because other than grace at Christmas and Easter, I had never prayed in front of anyone. The people in the new church we had been attending prayed for each other all the time. Their prayers weren't words I could memorize like the Hail Marys of my youth. Their prayers were specific requests; they were as personal as having a conversation with a trusted friend, and I had put my foot in my mouth more than once and hurt a trusted friend, so I was afraid I would say the wrong thing to God. I looked around Patrick's room. I wished I had a little candle to light, a small votive like the ones I lit for my mother.

Patrick closed his eyes and waited. His trust in me felt like a weight and wings at the same time. When I signed up for motherhood, I knew "play with your kids" was part of the job description, but no one said "pray with them" was on the list. I had prayed *for* my sons since they'd taken their tiny first breaths, but those prayers were private words. Words between God and me in the dark of night when my head was full of monsters and all the dangers of the world that could swallow them up.

"Mom?" Patrick lay flat on his back, hands folded on his chest. "I thought you said you were going to pray." His eyes were still closed, his face all scrunched up from squeezing them shut so tight, and little peeps blew out his nose as he concentrated.

I took a deep breath and started. "Dear God, can you please help Patrick sleep tonight? He's a good boy, and he needs his sleep so he can go to school." My words bolted out in a race to get to the finish line. Patrick opened one eye. His hands were still folded. "Is that all, Mom?" A car drove past the house, its headlights illuminating his bedroom. Our cat, Mittens, had found his favorite spot curled up at the foot of Patrick's bed, his steady purr as hypnotic as waves licking the shore.

"Oops, I guess I forgot the rest," I whispered. "Sorry, God." I cleared my throat. "Could you please help Patrick sleep *every* night?" I placed my hand atop Patrick's and waited to feel the familiar swell of air fill his lungs the same as I used to when he was a baby. "And could you please bless Michael and Mittens and Mozart and all of Patrick's friends . . . and his dad? Thank you, God, for your help. Amen."

Patrick slipped his hands under his covers and pulled the blanket up to his chin. He rolled on his side away from me, smacked his lips, and murmured, "Good night, Mom . . . and thanks." I caressed the top of his head, turned out his light, and closed the door behind me.

The next morning Patrick sat at the kitchen table, hunched over his bowl of Froot Loops, crunching louder than Mozart wolfing down his kibble.

"How did you sleep last night, honey?" I yawned and turned on the tap to fill the teakettle.

"I didn't wake up once, Mom." He flipped over a Pokémon card and placed it in his *got it* pile. "Why did you wait so long to pray for me?" He drained the pink milk from his cereal bowl, then stared at me, waiting for an answer.

"I guess I never thought about asking God to help

you sleep, Patrick. I thought we were supposed to only ask God for *big* things, honey. You know. Like starving children in Africa and stuff, things that are supposed to be God's to fix."

The kettle whistled, and I grabbed a mug from the cupboard. Patrick returned the box of Froot Loops to the pantry and stood beside me as I poured the steaming water into my cup. He wiped his mouth with his pajama sleeve and said, "Don't you know that God cares about every little thing, Mom? You should have prayed a long time ago!" He scooped his Pokémon cards off the table and ran upstairs to get dressed for school.

P.S. Your letters are being read in South Africa by a woman who wrote that her whole church is praying for your miracle. She's also forwarded them to family in Qatar, Bermuda, and Australia.

P.P.S. Where's Qatar?

> *And God heard them, for their*
> *prayer reached heaven.*
> —2 Chronicles 30:27

Wingless

Dear Deb,

Last weekend I met a young mother and her eighteen-month-old son, who were guests at the same cottage as me. She was tall and beautiful with flawless olive skin, the kind that looks sun kissed year-round. Not a blemish, freckle, or age spot in sight. Her young son had the same skin tone and sandy-haired curls that kissed his cheekbones and framed his dark chestnut eyes.

While she lazed against the bottom step of the sprawling porch of the century-old cottage, her son was fluid motion. Barefoot, he teetered from rock to rock in the hosta garden. He picked up stones along the path and patted the trunk of an ancient white pine. When he reached the gravel road and saw how it curved through the woods, he bolted like a puppy chasing a butterfly.

His mother hoisted herself up from the step and with a few long strides she gathered him in her arms and plunked him on her shoulders. She stood in front of me and swayed back and forth as he regarded the world from his high perch. "You know my son has something no one else has," she said. He giggled as she flipped him in a somersault over her head. Nestled into the bottom step once again with him on her lap, she rolled up the sleeve of his tiny striped T-shirt. She turned him around so his back faced me. "He has special dimples."

On the back of his shoulder, there was a small pucker, like someone had poked him. He had the same pucker on his other shoulder.

"What is that?" I asked. I had seen cheek dimples and dimples on lower backs but had never seen this before.

"I don't know, really," she said. "He was born with them." She hefted him over her shoulder. He grabbed a handful of her thick ponytail.

"Is there something missing with his bones or tissue that could have caused that?" I wondered if she'd had x-rays taken or seen a specialist.

"I don't think so. Guess what else?" she asked. She released her son, and he scooted up the steps on all fours to explore the porch. She twisted around to show me her back with the same dimples, one on each shoulder. Hers were a little larger, the size of a dime. "You see, we were born angels, and the doctors didn't know what to do with our wings." She smiled, and her eyes danced to the tune of her story. "So they snipped them off, and we were left with these marks."

"Oooh, I *love* that!" I said. "But don't you want to know if this is a genetic thing or something?"

She breezed past me to rescue her son, who had climbed up on an antique twig bench. "Nope," she answered. "I like it this way."

> *"For they are like the angels.*
> *They are God's children."*
> —Luke 20:36

Against All Odds

"Mr. Simmons, I need Miss Malcolmson in the office right away." Sister Magdalene's voice hissed through the classroom intercom. I was sitting on a lab stool in eleventh grade chemistry class. I had just poured a handful of broken spaghetti into a beaker of boiling water to see if it danced when I added vinegar. Mr. Simmons, aka the Michelin Man, had squeezed himself between my stool and the back wall and was close enough to rest his greasy chin on my shoulder. "Remember, girls, if an experiment *works*, something has gone wrong for sure." He laughed, spraying my cheek with breath that would make a dog cry. I was glad to be called away from his dog breath even though getting called to the principal's office was like getting called to the pearly gates when you weren't ready.

On my way to the office, I bumped into Tracy Newton coming out of the nurse's room. Tracy was one of the prettiest girls in high school and was as sweet as she was pretty. That day, she had another black eye. Everyone knew Tracy's father was wheelchair-bound, which was why no one could understand how she got in the way of his fists. But I knew why she didn't run from him.

Hope.

No matter what happened, she clung to the hope that this time it would be different. No matter how loud he roared, Tracy's hunger for her father's love was greater than her fear of his fists.

I knew a lot about that hope too.

I hoped I would be a good enough daughter to make my mother happy, and I hoped that one day I'd have a better life even though I had no idea what it would look like . . .

A few years ago I attended a seminar on perseverance. Perseverance has been a subject near and dear to my heart. We all fall down, and when we do it hurts. I've always wondered why some people can get up, brush themselves off, and move forward while others either stay on the ground or trudge along wearing their hurt like a life sentence. Whatever it was that helped people move forward, I wanted to make sure my sons had it.

The seminar was hosted by psychologists and social workers who had studied the lives of a control group of adults for thirty years. All of the adults in the study had one thing in common: horrific childhoods. Some grew up and went on to lead productive, successful lives. Others remained lost in their pasts. They ended up criminals, homeless, or in and out of psychiatric hospitals.

The research charted ten hallmarks most of us need

for stability and success, hallmarks that help develop perseverance. The list was handed to each participant in the study, who checked items that applied to his or her own life experience. Four hallmarks stood out. Every adult in the success group checked the same four items from the list of ten, stating them as key factors in contributing to their success:

1. a significant adult who told them they were special, one who believed in them (teachers, coaches, neighbors, relatives)
2. faith—a belief in something bigger than their circumstances
3. resilience—the ability to bounce back
4. hope—*a hope that there was a better life for them even though they didn't know what it would look like . . .*

As for me, I will always have hope.
—Psalm 71:14

Too Much Love?

Dear Deb,

I've been thinking about how often I say the word *love*.

I love goat cheese. I love antiques. I love Michael Bublé and bracelets that tinkle when I move my wrist. I also love goose down pillows, movies that make me weep, and an icy cold Corona on a hot day. I love my dog, and I love my sons.

Today, it occurred to me that I use the same word to describe both how I feel about my sons and how I feel about goat cheese. I thought I should learn other words to express all the variations of *love*, words that separate the kids from the cheese. I decided to check my thesaurus and discovered there are hundreds.

Cherish: No argument there. I cherish my down pillows when I fall into bed every night.

Fancy: Do I ever fancy goat cheese! I fancy it all

the time. On pizza, in salad, melted on a grilled steak, and sprinkled on strawberries.

Prefer: When it comes to beer, I prefer drinking my Corona from the bottle and with a wedge of lime, please. Serving me chips with guacamole would also make you a preferred friend!

Treasure: My desktop is made from a 120-year-old pine door with the original blue paint and a rathole gnawed at one end. I treasure those little teeth marks.

Adore: I adore my sons. I adore their generous hearts and their ability to forgive easily. But I love them too.

Embrace: Michael Bublé, yes. Anytime.

Prize: Viking is a prize pet even though he sheds more clumps of fur than a herd of buffalo.

Admire: I admire anyone who produces brilliant movies like *Steel Magnolias*, filled with characters that make me laugh and cry at the same time.

After I finished my list, I realized I'll probably never replace saying *love* with any of these words. *Love* sounds just right each time I say it. I can whisper it, sing it, or stretch it into two syllables. *Love* is a noun, a verb, an adjective, and an adverb. And no matter how it's used, it's something we all know. We love.

"She loved much."

—Luke 7:47

Thirty Days

Dear Deb,

"I'm sure some of you are here today who don't know why you're here. Maybe like a lot of people, you're looking for answers." Paul Johnson smiled as he fixed his gaze towards the back of the crowded church. With his polished complexion and thick, cropped auburn hair, he had one of those faces that defied age. He could have passed as the youth pastor instead of the founder of Woodridge Church, married twenty-five years with three children.

"You might believe in *something*, but you don't know what it is." He strolled across the stage with his hands clasped behind his back. A 12 x 12-foot screen suspended behind him showcased a photograph of a solitary man in climbing gear propped on a boulder that overlooked a vast sea of mountains. The music team had just finished a heart-swelling rendition of "You'll Never Walk Alone" with a female vocalist who belted it out better than Streisand.

"Some of you may come because you like the

music . . . I do, too, by the way! We are blessed with a great band." Everyone clapped and cheered for the band. Paul stood center stage and loosened his tie. A spotlight with an amber glow trailed him as he moved across the stage. "Perhaps your neighbor invited you for the sixth time and you finally came to get them to stop bugging you." A few people laughed as they exchanged glances. Behind me, a woman shushed a man who chuckled, "I'm here for the free coffee."

The door at the back of the church auditorium whined, and a soft streak of light poured into the aisle beside my seat. A volunteer from the nursery held a whimpering two-year-old in her arms. She canvassed the room for the parents as Paul pointed to a flip chart on the stage.

"Whether you know why you are here or not, I have a challenge for you," Paul announced. Behind him, the picture of the climber on the mountain peak was replaced with a gigantic thirty-day calendar. "I'd like you to use the next thirty days to try something that could change your life." He paused for effect, and we quieted like a crowd at a Broadway show instead of worshippers at a Sunday service.

I wondered where he was going with this. There had been many times in the past year I squirmed in my seat, convinced that Paul's words were directed at me alone. When he had talked about messy lives or how the sins of parents can follow their children, I had slumped down in my seat, worried that laser beams might shoot from his eyes and target me.

"I mean, what's thirty days?" He shrugged his

shoulders and paused. "Thirty days is four weeks, one month . . . one twelfth of a year!" He walked to the very edge of the stage. "I challenge all of you to take the next thirty days to act like a Christian." He walked off the stage.

The band regrouped and began to sing, "We Are One in the Spirit." Everyone stood up and sang along, voices building with the chorus. *"And they'll know we are Christians by our love, by our love . . ."*

I never dreamed I would ever stand shoulder to shoulder with a group of strangers singing hymns in a church. Especially these hymns with lyrics like country ballads that told stories of pain, of loss, and of a love bigger than any of us could imagine. I wondered if everyone was here for the same reason—to try to touch that love. I know I was.

"Did you know that James Taylor said he started out *pretending* to be a songwriter?" Paul returned when the song ended. "And look what happened from his 'pretending'!" He paused and smiled. "I'll bet everyone in this room has heard 'You've Got a Friend' more than once. I'll bet, too, that before that song was born, James Taylor practiced writing and strumming until his fingers were bloodied and his throat felt like sandpaper." Paul walked towards the edge of the stage. "Starting today, why don't you take the thirty-day challenge? Go home and act like a Christian." He grinned and opened his arms wider than an opera singer at an ovation. "Love each other . . . do something for someone else . . . and pray."

Chatter bubbled up like a creek after a spring thaw as people prepared to go home to Sunday brunch. I stood up to put my coat on, and I wondered what the heck he meant. How was *acting* like a Christian the same as *pretending* to be a songwriter? I thought it was weird that Paul didn't include any rules in his challenge. Like going to church on Sundays. Or reading the Bible. Most challenges had rules, lines drawn in the sand, that we weren't allowed to cross.

That night, I went for a walk and noticed a bunch of neighborhood kids singing and giggling while they skipped in circles around a lamppost. A little girl tripped and fell, and without missing a beat, another girl rushed to her side to help her up. She knelt down to inspect her knee. I watched as she leaned forward and blew on the tiny scrape, something I'd done for my own sons after a fall. A thought occurred to me then, about Paul's message: *Maybe the only rule for his challenge was kindness . . .*

> *Faith by itself, if it is not*
> *accompanied by action, is dead.*
>
> —James 2:17

The Confession

Dear Deb,

"I know I have to tell you this stuff, Mom, but I'm afraid you're going to hate me when you hear it." Michael talked to his feet while he slid the zipper of his hooded sweatshirt up and down. He was sitting beside me in the passenger seat of my road-weary SUV.

"No matter what you tell me, I'm not going to hate you, honey. I love you and am so proud of you for doing the work to fix yourself." I backed out of our driveway and smiled at him, hoping to portray a courage I didn't feel. "I can't imagine how hard this is for you, living in that place." I patted his shoulder.

Michael had the face of an angel with sea green eyes and long, dark lashes Maybelline could use to sell mascara. The patchy stubble shadowing the hollows of his cheeks reminded me of a kindergarten self-portrait where he glued sand to his face to appear grown-up. He had wanted to be "big" since he was two years old. Now, a few months after his nineteenth birthday, we were headed back to the Portage Centre, where he was a resident with twenty-seven other drug addicts. He had earned his first twelve-hour pass after two months of rehab that had felt like a prison term to all of us.

While he visited his brother and me at home, he was required to complete an assignment. He was supposed to disclose the intimate details of his drug use and record our reactions and feelings about them. The first few hours of his pass, he wandered from room to room checking to see if everything at home was the same as he'd left it. He reminded me of our dog sniffing out each room after a lengthy kennel stay. Michael spent some time on his computer, played a few video games with Patrick, then plopped himself in front of the television in the family room next to the kitchen.

"Man, I haven't watched TV in so long . . ." He tuned in to *The Simpsons*, a family favorite. "Oh, I love this show . . ."

"Dinner will be ready in about fifteen minutes." I pulled the roast chicken out of the oven and placed it on the counter to set. My mouth watered when I lifted its foil, and I breathed in the scents of rosemary, lemon, and garlic. I set three places at the table and lit a few candles. Every step of Michael's recovery was a celebration. I hesitated before I laid a napkin beside his plate. My chest hurt, and I realized I was holding my breath. This was the first time in months I was setting the table for the three of us. Michael had left us long before he entered rehab. He had been lost to the streets for weeks before he was ready to accept help, and no matter how brave I tried to be with him living in a treatment facility, seeing his empty chair at dinner each night made me crumble. Looking at his chair brought back memories of the late-night phone calls, the ambulances, the overdoses. We were lucky. The statistics for saving young adults hooked on crack were grim. If Michael hadn't been willing to commit to rehab, his chair might have been empty forever. I lost my balance and leaned against the table for support. Guilt and panic had been bullying me since I discovered Michael was using.

I shouldn't have moved from Minnesota.

What if he had almost died because I moved us back to Canada?

Breathe, I commanded. *Michael is alive and home. For now. That's all that counts. The now.*

I hung on to the fridge door and prayed the same prayer I had prayed a thousand times. *"Please, God, heal my son. Keep him at Portage until he can live without drugs. Help him find the same beautiful Michael he lost."* I chugged a glass of water, hoping it would drown the guilt. I threw a green salad together, carved the chicken, and prepared the potatoes, pounding them with the masher until my arm ached.

"Man, these potatoes are so good. You have no idea how many times I ate cold mashed potatoes in the last two months." Michael hovered four inches above his plate, wolfing down his dinner like he had been living in the wild.

The kitchen was bathed in amber light from the

votive candles on the table and windowsills, a stark contrast to the starless January night. Michael Bublé crooned "Try a Little Tenderness" in the background. Normal. I wanted everything normal when nothing was normal.

Patrick scarfed down a piece of chicken breast. A spot of gravy clung to his chin. "Do you have to do the cooking in there?" He talked to his plate. It had been a year since he looked Michael in the eyes. Michael had been his idol, the big brother who could answer every question he threw at him, the big brother who had loved spending time with him until drugs became Michael's only friend.

"Yeah, but it's not *real* cooking. Everything is instant, from a box . . . total crap."

Michael pushed his plate towards the center of the table. It was as spotless as if the dog had licked it clean. He grabbed a chocolate chip cookie, still warm from the oven, and leaned back in his chair.

"Most of the food comes from Corrections; did you know that? Jail food. Potatoes are instant too . . . disgusting crap." He chugged his milk and wiped his mouth on his sleeve.

Patrick pushed his plate away unfinished. "Si-i-i-ick." He folded his arms across his chest.

I didn't care where the food came from. Michael had gained ten pounds in two months and looked healthier than he had in two years. Drugs have a calling card that reads: "If you want to lose everything, call me." Michael had lost two years of high school, a few jobs, and twenty-five pounds. With more than one overdose, he had almost lost his life.

Turned out Michael couldn't bring himself to complete his assignment in front of his brother. He waited until the last moment to fess up in the car with me. By that time, I was more worried about the drive back to the Portage Centre than about his confession. We hadn't had much snow in southern Ontario for January, but Elora, a small country village ninety minutes north of us, was more like the Midwest with drifts piled high along the sides of the roads like snow steeples.

"You are going to hate me for sure when I tell you, Mom." We had been driving for almost an hour. He had shared a few stories about the other residents and how they landed at Portage when I reminded him that he was supposed to be discussing his own drug history.

"I hate me now." He moaned. "And I'll bet God even hates me, Mom." I wanted to wrap my arms around him, but I knew his shame was a part of his healing I couldn't protect him from. I reached over the console and placed my palm on his cheek. I wanted to be a sponge so I could absorb all his pain.

"I'll bet you've never done anything horrible that you can't take back. So how are you ever going to understand how I feel?" He faced me, mouth twisted and eyes so mournful I wanted to hunt down every drug dealer in the country, crucify them, and line them up along the trans-Canada highway like the Romans did to the slaves on the Appian Way. If he only knew some of the things I've done in my life that I couldn't take back. But the only me that Michael knew was Mom, feeding his needs since he was born. I held his handsome face for a moment, recalling the many times I cradled him when he was a toddler. I yearned for those days when the most daring leap Michael made was off the dock at Rooney Lake.

I pulled over to the edge of a field on the country road to face Michael. The night was murky black with the cloud cover a silent thief that had stolen the moon and the stars. As we sat in the middle of farm country without a house or convenience store in sight, I remembered my own mistake that I couldn't take back.

"I do know how it feels to do something that you can't take back, Michael." I leaned back against the headrest.

"What could you have possibly done, Mom?" he asked. "Smoked marijuana in the sixties? Everyone did that." He looked out the passenger window, and I followed his gaze. A few feeble cornstalks poked through the snowdrifts. The car engine shimmied and whined in high gear like a colt anxious to bolt. I inhaled as much air as my lungs could hold, like I was jumping into the deep end, and I prayed. *Thank you, God, for saving my son and keeping him in this place until he heals. Please give me the right words to say to him now. Words that will help him know he's not the only one who has made mistakes. Words that will let him know there is nothing he could do that could make me stop loving him.*

Michael wriggled himself up as tall as his 5'8" frame allowed with his seat belt still attached. He looked down at his lap and let his hands fall limp at the sides of the bucket seats. These past two years, friends asked me how I could forgive Michael for the overdoses, the sleepless nights, the stealing. They didn't understand there was nothing to forgive; there was nothing Michael could do that could make me love him less. He was my bright shiny star whose light went out for a while, and I would do anything to help him light it again. If my own confession would help him see that we all make mistakes and our mistakes don't have to define us, I would tell him about mine. I wanted him to believe God had a better life for him, just like he did for me.

On a country road on the darkest winter night, I confessed a mistake from my past that had haunted me for years. A mistake I couldn't make right. And Michael confessed to me.

He chewed on his cheek, but it didn't stop his tears that were like rain on his face. "I'm glad you told me that, Mom." He dragged his arm across his face to wipe his nose on his sleeve, then sputtered and grinned as soon as he realized what he had done. "I don't know how to say this, but I love you more now than I ever thought I could love anybody." He threw his arms around my neck and clung to me with the same gusto as the little boy I cradled in my arms in the deep end of Rooney Lake, the little boy who learned to trust me enough to let go to swim on his own.

"You know, Mom, I couldn't do any of this without you and Patrick loving me. It's the only thing I have right now that keeps me going." He rubbed his eyes with the butt of his hands like he was rubbing out a mistake with an eraser.

It was harder to let go of Michael that night than it was when I'd dropped him off two months earlier. Maybe it was because I was so desperate to save his life back then that I was ready to hand him over to any savior available. Or maybe it was the look on his face when he glanced back to smile at me. Something had changed. There was a tiny light in his eyes that reminded me of Michael before drugs. And there was a single tear. It wound around the curve of his cheek and rested in the hollow. *Bye, Mom,* he mouthed. He turned to walk up the steps. When he reached the front door of the center, he didn't look back. Instead he waved over his shoulder. It was the same wave he gave me summer mornings at the cabin after he'd gulp the last of my tea—the mornings he'd waved over his shoulder just before he leapt off the dock to swim in the crystal waters of Rooney Lake.

Therefore confess your sins to each other and
pray for each other so that you may be healed.
—James 5:16

Stones in My Shoes

Dear Deb,

I have always had narrow feet. When I was a girl, I was a poster child for the fashion statement *If the shoe fits, it's ugly.* The only shoes I could wear had to be laced so they wouldn't flop off or chafe against my heels. Even the best Hush Puppies were loose on me, and no matter how tight I tied the laces, their sides gaped wide enough to fit my finger, a nice little pocket for stray stones. At the end of every day, I would slip off my shoes and turn them upside down to shake out the stones that were nesting under my feet. Sometimes a big stone would sneak in, and I'd have to stop playing to remove it right away. Other times I'd ignore the irritation only to discover my sock bloodied where a stone had rubbed my skin raw. We are such funny creatures, Deb. I can't count how many times I've endured pain because of a single stone when all I had to do was admit it hurt. Pride. Youth. And caring too much about appearances.

I am happy to say I finally grew into my feet, and today I have more shoe options. Red shoes, blue shoes, strappy sandals, shoes with bling, open-toed, slingbacks, slip-ons, I love them all! But no matter how great they look or how well they fit, there are times I still get stones in them. The difference now is I don't ever wait until a stone makes me bleed. I stop, shake out my shoes, and continue to go forward. Ahhh, the advantages of aging and learning lessons the hard way. This little story tells it best . . .

A lecturer, when explaining stress management to an audience, raised a glass of water and asked, "How heavy is this glass of water?" Answers called out ranged from 20g to 500g.

The lecturer replied, "The absolute weight doesn't matter. It depends on how long you try to hold it. If I hold it for a minute, that's not a problem. If I hold it for an hour, I'll have an ache in my right arm. If I hold it for a day, you'll have to call an ambulance. In each case, it's the same weight, but the longer I hold it, the heavier it becomes." He continued, "And that's the way it is with stress management. If we carry our burdens all the time, sooner or later, as the burden becomes increasingly heavy, we won't be able to carry on."†

---

† Adapted from http://www.holybible.com/resources/poems/ps.php?sid=1131.

P.S. I hope you get to shake your shoes out tonight, Deb. I heard they're a bit full of stones.

"Come to me, all you who are weary and burdened, and I will give you rest."
—Matthew 11:28

Time for Lunch

Dear Deb,

After visiting a friend in Toronto, I stopped at my favorite restaurant on Queen Street West for lunch. I've never been comfortable eating alone in restaurants, but I refuse to let that stop me from trying new places. I've learned to take a book with me. When I'm reading I'm never alone. I've had some great dinners with Holden Caulfield, Miss Havisham, and Detective Lucas Davenport.

At the restaurant, I found a small window table in a quiet corner. The noon sun spilled across the tabletop, providing ample light to read. I ordered a glass of Chianti and the Santo Stefano pizza: buffalo mozzarella and sliced tomato on a thin, crispy crust topped with a handful of fresh arugula and prosciutto di Parma. My mouth watered as I remembered the last time I had ordered the same thing. The salty ham mixed with bitter greens and sweet cheese was heaven on a plate. I sipped my Chianti and relaxed into my cozy nook to read and wait for my lunch to arrive.

I had finished one page when two young mothers sat at the table next to me with four toddlers. I smiled at them as they arranged booster seats, poured little mounds of fish crackers in front of each child, and emptied toys and coloring books from their backpacks. Throughout lunch my cozy corner was filled with birdsong voices of little ones singing "Old MacDonald Had a Farm." The mothers rescued pizza from the floor, wiped red sauce out of stinging eyes, and commanded over and over to each child to "sit still!" It didn't help. The kids continued bouncing up and down like a quartet of jack-in-the-boxes.

Watching the antics at the table and the mothers' attempts to sip their frothy lattes without interruption was better drama than my book. It made me yearn for the days when I took my own sons on restaurant adventures. I missed seeing their little teeth marks in my grilled cheese sandwich and their slobber on my glass of Diet Coke.

As they packed up to leave, one mother looked at me and said, "My friend and I have been watching you throughout our lunch. We're both so jealous that you could be out enjoying a meal alone with a glass of wine." She stuffed a toy fire engine into her pack and sighed. "I would give anything to have a meal alone." Her son raced to the door, and she ran to catch him.

There is a time for everything, and a season
for every activity under the heavens.

—Ecclesiastes 3:1

Who's Your Graeme?

Dear Deb,

Now that I'm an empty nester and live alone, I often suffer from hug withdrawal. On those days I head over to my sister Lisa's to get a fix. I walk in the front door, drop my purse on the floor, and call from the foyer, "Aunty Margie needs a hug!" Her eight-year-old son, Owen, flies upstairs and throws his whole self against me. He wraps his arms around my waist and squeezes me with all his big boy might. As I hug him back, I say, "Thank you, sweetie; you are the best hugger in the world," which makes him squeeze me even harder. Sometimes I make a pretend crying voice and wail, "I miss hugging Michael and Patrick!" and when I do that Owen presses his freckled cheek against my tummy and tells me he loves me.

A few weeks ago I was visiting Lisa's family when her five-year-old daughter, Sarah, approached me. "Can I sit with you, Aunty Margie?"

The overstuffed chair in their family room made a comfy cocoon for cuddles and reading stories. I opened my arms wide, and Sarah navigated the chair with the finesse of a gymnast. She curled into my lap, pulled her knees up to her chest, and tucked her head under my chin. Her shoulder-length chestnut curls were damp, a few ringlets glued to her forehead. Her hair smelled like a new puppy. I twirled her downy strands around my fingers, something that felt as natural as breathing. The two of us sat there without speaking for a few moments, content with the rhythms of our heartbeats.

Lisa prepared dinner in the kitchen. We could hear her opening and closing cupboards, chopping vegetables. "You want to stay for dinner?" she called over the sounds of rushing water from a pot she was filling. I loved that invitation. Lisa's simplest meals were better than most gourmet restaurants'.

"Aunty Margie?" Sarah slipped off my ring and slid it down her thumb. "Who is your graeme?" She tried the ring on each of her fingers before she placed it back on her thumb. She spun it like a toy.

"What do you mean, honey?" Graeme was her dad. He was working downstairs in his home office.

"Who is your graeme?" she repeated. She sat up to face me.

"You mean who is my *dad*?" I asked. "My dad is your grandpa, honey." I remembered my own sons being confused about family relationships and titles when they were young. Who belonged to whom was complicated when you were five.

"No . . . your *graeme*," she insisted. "Do you have one?" Sarah fixed her dark eyes on me and waited.

"You mean a husband, honey? A man for me like your dad is for your mommy?"

"Yes . . . your graeme!" Her face lit up. "Who is he?" She chewed her bottom lip.

"I don't have a graeme, sweetie. Aunty Margie lives by herself."

Sarah fell against me and tucked her head under my chin again. She sighed a deep sigh that took all of her breath. "It makes me sad that you live by yourself now." She toyed with the top buttons on my blouse.

"I know," I said. "Sometimes it makes me sad too, honey." I wrapped my arms around her and stroked her silky hair over and over . . .

"Yet I am not alone, for my Father is with me."
—John 16:32

Five Smooth Stones

Dear Deb,

My dad was right when he called me a dreamer. I still have some of the weirdest dreams and sometimes wake up with recall that's as clear as seeing an adventure movie on the big screen. This morning I woke up after a dream about David and Goliath. I had no idea if I was supposed to be David or the ugly giant or why I'd even dream about them. *Lord, I need to get out more!* I thought. I tried to concentrate on my morning visitors and what I'd serve for brunch, but as I tidied my kitchen, I had an itch that wouldn't go away. I sat down with my steaming cup of coffee and tried to figure out what was bugging me. Why couldn't I stop thinking about David and Goliath? I looked up the story in my Bible to see if it could tell me.

> *[David] chose five smooth stones from the stream, put them in the pouch of his shepherd's bag and, with his sling in his hand, approached the [giant]. (1 Samuel 17:40)*

There it was.

Five smooth stones.

Why five? Why not ten? What about buckets of stones? David was a teenager, and the other guy was a GIANT, after all. And why smooth stones and not ragged rocks? Wouldn't they hurt more?

I get frustrated when I read a detail like that in any story and the author fails to explain its significance. Most times I can overlook it and let myself be carried by the flow of the story, but when it comes to the Bible, I always think there has to be a reason for every detail or else it wouldn't be there.

Thank heavens for Google. Google knows everything. Here are five explanations I found:

- The five smooth stones represent David's faith. The stones were tried and true. He had confidence in them. Having used them before to protect his flock, he knew what the outcome would be. He also had four in reserve to be prepared. What if the first stone David threw had missed the giant?
- Goliath had four brothers, BIGGER ones.
- The stones represent Ephesians 4:11: "some to be apostles, some to be prophets, some to be evangelists, and some to be pastors and teachers."
- The five smooth stones symbolize things that help us deal with our lives: prayer, hope, love, faith, trust.
- The five stones represent the sides of the pentagon building in Washington, a war machine prophecy. *(Ha-ha . . . can you believe this one, Deb?)*

After reading over twenty articles on the significance of the five smooth stones, it seems no one really knows for sure. Maybe the stones are one of those details God helped the writer capture because he thought it was important. Maybe its importance is that it would keep us talking and wondering a few thousand years later. I'm not sure. But those stones sure got me thinking . . .

Mother Teresa said, "I know God will not give me anything I can't handle. I just wish that He didn't trust me so much." Whether David used five stones or twenty, I think the story shows how God trusted a teenage shepherd boy to perform an incredible task. And it shows how that teenage boy trusted him.

> *"If you have faith as small as a mustard*
> *seed . . . nothing will be impossible for you."*
> —Matthew 17:20

Red Jacket Guy

Dear Deb,

On a Monday I noticed his bright red jacket, bold as a stop sign stretched across his bulging belly. I thought he was a high school student the way he strode toward us swinging his arms up and down like he was in a marching band. But with his baseball cap tugged low on his forehead, tufts of snowy white hair spilled over his ears and betrayed his age.

"Look at this old guy, Patrick!" I said. "He's zooming along like he's in a marathon . . . Look at his face, Mr. Happy . . . ha, ha!"

Patrick lay back against the headrest of the car, eyes closed, half-eaten bagel in hand, his morning posture when I drove him to Nelson High School. "No . . . talking . . . pleeeeeze." He reached back to flip up the hood attached to his jacket. He yanked it down over his eyes like a shroud.

As I approached Mr. Happy, I gave the horn a little toot-toot and waved. He stopped mid-stride and squinted as we drove past. His breath was frosty clouds that he shooed away as he watched us drive by.

"Who's that?" Patrick stirred. He tore into his bagel.

"I dunno . . . some old man walking down the street. I've never seen him before."

"Why'd you wave at him?"

"He just looked like someone worth waving at." I laughed when I realized I was doing the same thing my father had done when I was a teenager. Embarrassed me to death. He'd wave at strangers, roll the window down, and stick his head out and say, "Hey pal . . . how the hell are ya?"

"You're weird, Mom." Patrick rolled his eyes.

The next morning Mr. Happy marched towards us again. I honked and waved. He stopped and squinted. Patrick rolled his eyes.

On Thursday Mr. Happy waved back.

Patrick said "No way," and sat up to watch him over his shoulder. "Man, his jacket is really red, Mom."

He renamed him "Red Jacket Guy."

Every school morning that fall, Red Jacket Guy paraded towards us. I honked and waved, and he waved back. Patrick stopped pulling his hood over his eyes and started watching out for Red Jacket Guy. "Here he comes, Mom!" he'd exclaim. "Look how he's pumpin' his arms—the guy's on a mission." But Patrick would never acknowledge him. Waving wasn't cool.

One day Red Jacket Guy waved at me before I honked.

For six months each weekday morning, we waved and smiled at each other, old friends marking our daily routines. In early May just before the buds on the trees stretched into leaves, Patrick finally lifted his hand and placed his open palm against the window. He nodded to Red Jacket Guy. Red Jacket Guy nodded back.

P.S. Am thinking today of all the foreign students you hosted, Deb. Lucky them.

> *Do not forget to entertain strangers, for*
> *by so doing some people have entertained*
> *angels without knowing it.*
>
> —Hebrews 13:2

Heart's Desire

Dear Deb,

The other day a friend asked, "What's your heart's desire?" Since I've never had a difficult time with *wanting*, a million things raced through my mind, a weekend with George Clooney being at the top of the list. A shopping trip to Paris and a vacation were next. My sons and I haven't had a family vacation since we moved to Canada in 2003. How I would love to take them somewhere, just the three of us, without work, cell phones, or computers! I yearned for the closeness we had all those summers on Rooney Lake.

Finishing and selling my memoir, huge desire. I can't imagine how it would feel to hold *The Painted Couch* in my hand, to turn each page, caress each hard-earned word and read the last line over and over. And if I'm going to list desires, I'd like Oprah and two million other readers to do the same thing. Definitely up there with the weekend with George. Financial security made the initial list, too, but I swept it away because worrying about money gives me a rash.

As I was listing all the things my heart desires faster than a six-year-old recites the ABCs, my friend stopped me and said, "I don't mean things you *want*, Margaret." He rolled his eyes. "We all want a vacation." He explained that heart's desire is more than wanting. Heart's desire is that thing on the road ahead that offers the life I hope to have. It's the thing that will feed my heart and spirit until they overflow with unimaginable peace. My inside voice almost spilled out, *George Clooney could do a very nice job of feeding my heart, thank you very much*, but I put a lid on that voice and told my friend I needed time to think about it.

For days, I asked my heart over and over, *What is on the road ahead that you want and don't have? What is there waiting for you that you might trip over and not see because you are too busy with your lists and your life?*

One morning I woke up, and I knew what it was.

Freedom.

My heart wants the freedom to be a writer without restraints, the freedom to love again without fear, and the freedom to hear God without my insecure self getting in the way.

Yup, freedom would feed my heart and give me peace.

> *May he give you the desire of your heart*
> *and make all your plans succeed.*
>
> —Psalm 20:4–5

Going Home

Dear Deb,

My sister Lisa strolled through the front door, flaunting a plate of homemade raspberry muffins warm from her oven. January's chill was right behind her, and I shivered when the biting air sliced through my polar fleece robe.

"I made some love for you!" Lisa sang as she kicked off her boots and passed the muffins to me. The fusion of cinnamon, nutmeg, and brown sugar overwhelmed me with a yearning for Rooney Lake that gripped my heart. That same spicy aroma filled the cabin when I baked the boys' favorite cinnamon buns each summer. I hadn't baked anything since I'd sold the cabin to move back to Canada.

I turned on my coffeemaker as Lisa slid into a leather armchair with a back high as a king's throne. She was wearing her favorite wooly cardigan over her red flannel pajamas with the skating penguins. With her hair tied in a ponytail and the sprinkling of fawn freckles across her nose, she looked like a teenager instead of a thirty-five-year-old mom with a young son.

"Why would God let this happen to you?" Lisa crossed her arms and kneaded her shoulders. She winced when she tried to mold her back into the chair. The distressed leather fooled everyone into thinking the chairs were marshmallow soft.

"I don't think God *let* this happen, Lisa. I was the one who fell in love and accepted a marriage proposal. I also made the decision to move here." The coffeemaker whirred and sputtered. I picked at the crumble topping on a muffin. "I'm sorry, honey. I just can't eat anything right now. I know you got up early to make these for me. They look very Martha Stewart with those juicy raspberries poking out the top." I pushed the plate towards her and looked out the window at the new landscape that had been my home for the last six months. A row of stately houses faced me on the other side of a wide grassy boulevard the length of a football field. The street was lined with ancient maples the town protected under their historical trees act. It would take three adults with wide-open arms to encircle the trunk of the gigantic tree bordering my property.

"I know you're the one who made the decision to move back, Margie, but look what it cost you. You were supposed to have a wonderful new life, and now it's a big mess!" Lisa had been my biggest supporter of the decision to move back to Canada, excited to have me living in the same town as her after being away for twenty years.

The coffeemaker beeped its ready signal, and she

jumped up to fill our mugs. Her ponytail bounced behind her like a tetherball. "It's not fair. Michael and Patrick are suffering too. Why would God let them get hurt again?"

I was surprised how easily Lisa talked about God. Until three years ago, I didn't even say his name out loud. Lisa talked about him like he was a neighbor who lived down the street.

"I thought after praying about this with all your holy friends in Minnesota, you were sure it was the right thing to do, sure that he was 'the one.' I just don't get how this could happen." She set the steaming mugs on the table and popped a sugar-coated raspberry in her mouth.

I stood up to stretch my back. My neck muscles felt as though they had fossilized. I nodded my head up and down in an attempt to soften the knot that caused me to walk stiff as a runway model. "Did you think because I became a Christian my life was gonna be perfect?"

"No . . . I didn't think your life was going to be *perfect*, perfect. Nothing's perfect—I know that—but I thought God was supposed to be on your side now that you go to church and all that." A long curl freed itself from her ponytail. She wrapped it around her finger and twirled it round and round. "Come on, Margie. Haven't you been through enough with the divorce and everything? Where is God in all this?"

I sat back down and faced her. Lisa asked the same question I had been asking every night. Where *was* God in all of this? I had sold our family home and the cabin for love and a new beginning in Canada, but before the boxes were unpacked, I knew I had made a mistake. A few short months after our arrival in Canada, I ended the relationship and cancelled the wedding. Michael and Patrick were devastated and felt like they had left their friends and life behind for nothing. I felt like I had failed them again.

"I don't know where God is in this, honey. Maybe God wanted me here, and this was a way to make it happen." I sipped my coffee. "I don't know—I wish I knew how God worked. If I had known this was going to happen, I never would have moved."

Lisa slipped the rubber band from her ponytail and whipped her head back and forth. Her thick, auburn hair streaked with copper highlights tumbled below her shoulders. I had missed her all those years in Minnesota. No matter how crushed I was over my mistake to fall in love with the wrong person, I was happy Lisa and I could be a real family at this stage in our lives. I looked forward to sharing day-to-day life with her, dropping in for a visit, seeing her face more than once a year.

"You should be mad at God, Margie. I'm a little mad, and I hardly know him!" Lisa folded her arms over her chest. "You had a good life in Minnesota, and you were doing so well. Look how far you came since the divorce. You had friends, your church, and what about the cabin? You *loved* Rooney Lake." She chewed on her bottom lip. "Now you have to start all over. It's just not fair!" The youngest of the five sisters, Lisa had maintained a child-like sweetness, yet she was a fierce champion of right and wrong.

"I know you aren't going to understand this, honey,

but I don't blame God." I sighed. "Maybe I don't blame him because I need him right now. I need to believe there's a reason why we moved here, and I need to believe that one day I'll know what it is." I laid my cheek on the weathered pine table, the surface cool and stable. I wondered how many tears this table had absorbed, how many angry fists. The French Canadian dealer told me it was almost 135 years old, yet it was strong and secure on legs three times as old as mine.

Lisa reached across the table and grabbed my hands. "I love, love that you are here. I'm thrilled we get to do life together, that you will know my son and I can get close to Michael and Patrick." She squeezed my fingers. "But the cost has been terrible. I hate seeing you hurt again."

The cost *was* high. I moved Michael and Patrick a thousand miles away from their childhood home and gave up my financial support and friends for a love that was smoke and mirrors. I just had to believe God had something else in mind for us here. If I didn't, I would lose it. No matter how lousy it was right now, I believed in my heart everything would work out. How would I explain to Lisa I trusted something I couldn't see?

"Remember when I was going through the divorce and my friend Ruth sent me that Christmas card with the Bible quote and I had no idea what it meant? And then, I found that painting in the antique shop?" I pointed to the wall behind me where it hung. *With God Nothing Shall Be Impossible.* It was the only painting I'd hung so far. "Well, something happened to me that day that was as exciting as those first stages of falling in love. You know that wild butterflies-in-your-stomach feeling when you think about a new love?"

Lisa raised her eyebrows. "You mean the feeling that made you agree to get married in the first place?" She scrunched up her face like she was changing a dirty diaper.

"Ha-ha. Yeah, I guess so." I peeled the paper skirt off a muffin and broke it in half. "But this is different. It's better than falling in love, honey. After I saw that painting, I decided there was no such thing as a coincidence. It was just too big to ignore. I really, really believe God put that painting in that store for me. Or that he led me to it somehow—I don't know how all that stuff works with God. But I think he was trying to get my attention—it still boggles my mind."

Lisa fixed her lips in a tight line and squinted her eyes like she was trying to see in the dark.

"Anyways," I continued, "I made a choice then, you know . . . to believe he was real. God, I mean. That he was in charge of everything and that if he loved me as much as Ruth said, everything would turn out the way it was supposed to."

Lisa strode over to the sink. She started to wipe the counter even though it was clean. "OK—I can buy all that. I'm glad you have God to help you cope right now, but you still have big problems, Margie," she said. "This house is way too expensive, and you have no income. What are you going to do?"

"I need to find a church," I announced. I hadn't been to church since we moved. Talking about Ruth made me miss her and miss my faith family. "The boys need a church too. They made a lot of friends at the last one, and I think it'll help all of us feel like we belong here."

After Lisa left, I headed for the basement to empty a few more boxes. Even though it had been six months in the new house, I had only unpacked the basics. All the little extras that make a house a home had been stuck in limbo like me. I stood in front of a half dozen boxes marked "books" and felt a tug in my heart that made my throat ache. *My books!* I missed them! How could I have left them down here so long, their voices smothered in a dark box? It was funny the connection I felt to my books, especially since I didn't read any until my midtwenties. I had been the storyteller in my family, not the reader. Maybe that's why I felt so attached to them. Someone cared enough to take the time to tell *me* a story. I hefted a box to the floor, ripped off the tape, and flipped the lid back. The scent of aged cardboard and paper took me back to my favorite book-store in Minnesota, the one attached to the coffee shop where Ruth and I'd had that first coffee. Ruth. She loved me no matter how many crazy stories I told her about my life. Or how many times I cross-examined her about why Jesus talked in riddles instead of just saying what he meant. Ruth held my hand and helped me let go of the control I thought I needed to feel safe, and she introduced me to the one person I could trust.

"Why do you care whether I know God or not?" I had challenged after our first meeting. "What's it to you?"

Ruth smiled at me and held her purse against her chest like a schoolgirl holding an armful of books. She didn't quote the Bible, and she didn't lecture me about saving my soul. She answered so softly I had to strain to hear her.

"Oh, Margaret." Her eyes had misted as she stepped closer and placed a hand on my shoulder. "So you know how much you are loved."

P.S. I love you, Deb. And God loves you more.

Love, Margaret

> *And now these three remain: faith, hope,*
> *and love. But the greatest of these is love.*
> —1 Corinthians 13:13

The Miracles

Dear Reader,

Faith is a funny thing. Most people want it, and those who have it wish they had more. It's something we try to measure, which is like a child asking a parent, "How much do you love me?"

"Up to the sky," I'd say to Patrick when he asked. "To the moon and back," I'd tell Michael.

Deb had *up to the sky, to the moon and back* faith. When she announced, "I'm going to have a miracle," she didn't know what it would be, only that she was going to have one. Deb didn't say, "I *need* a miracle," which is what I would have said and what I was thinking after she shared her diagnosis. She said, "I'm going to have one." And she never stopped believing it.

Deb's faith in her miracle was infectious. I caught it and didn't know it until I wrote in one of her letters, "I believe in your miracle." When her letters traveled the world, other people caught it too. Hundreds of strangers wrote with the same message. *I believe.* Maybe that was her miracle. Or maybe it was just one of them. For the six months I wrote to her, I hoped her miracle would be that her cancer was cured. But that was the one *I* wanted, not the one God had in mind when he whispered those words to her. And that's the part of faith that's so hard. The trust. It's the part I forget about when I put so much of my heart into believing. Deb knew about trust, though. She trusted God to give her a miracle whether she lived to see it or not. Writing to her taught me that when faith holds hands with trust, miracles can happen.

Once I started believing in Deb's miracle, I started believing in me too. Writing to her helped me give voice to secrets that had been hiding in shame for too many years. I learned that no matter how terrified I was to be nakedly honest about my mistakes and my hopes and dreams, vulnerability is a quality that opens doors to beautiful friendships. I learned that the most tender, private things in our hearts have the most universal appeal and can connect us to strangers in wondrous ways. Faith is a funny thing.

Ten days before Deb died, she sat at her kitchen table while I made us toasted tomato sandwiches with sharp Canadian cheddar cheese. She gave orders like a Hollywood director as she supervised each step of the sandwich making. "You might need to put the bread in the toaster twice. I like the toast to be toast. Don't forget lots of mayo and pepper—I love pepper." Throughout lunch, Deb bubbled over with childhood stories. She laughed when she recalled her family with six siblings driving across Canada in a station wagon and how she sat on the backseat floor and read books the whole trip. "I was the oldest of seven kids and never wanted to be the oldest—when I was younger, I used to wish I was an only child." She grinned with the memory of childhood fantasies. "I was a huge reader. I read books and stories everywhere, even in the bathroom—it was the only place I had to be alone." Deb had the most striking blue eyes that bathed her face in light, eyes that looked like they were always ready to laugh. "Reading was my escape." She sighed. I sat across from her and held her hand as she continued to share childhood adventures—it was Deb's moment to remember things worth remembering.

Just before I left that afternoon, she asked me to fetch her letters and the comments from readers I had printed and given her a few days earlier. She had kept them on a small table next to the hospital bed that had been installed in her living room.

"I have to tell you something." She laid her hand on the stack of curled pages I placed in front of her. She caressed them like she was reading Braille.

"Some days when I read your letters, it was as though you knew exactly how I felt." She smiled a crooked smile, her face swollen and dehydrated from massive doses of steroids and toxic medications. "I thought you were writing stories just for me, until I read these comments and saw how many other people needed them too." Her voice was barely a whisper. After our three-hour visit, she had run out of gas.

I stood to leave, but she held up her hand like a policeman ordering traffic to stop. She hadn't finished what she wanted to say and was digging deep to find the breath to continue.

"I just want you to know . . ." She coughed a deep, wet cough and held on to her chest.

I was about to tell her that whatever she had to say could wait until next time, but her eyes told me *now* was the time.

"I want you to know," she repeated, "that if my illness inspired you to write these stories, the cancer was worth it." She fell back into her chair and smiled at me, satisfied at the victory of finishing the sentence.

It was my turn to struggle for air. My first reaction was to disagree vehemently and tell her there's *nothing* that can make cancer worth it. But I didn't. I didn't say a word. Something told me Deb was holding on and letting go at the same time, and I needed to accept this grace, this offering that was bigger than me, so I did the only thing I could think of: I laid my hand on top of hers, and for the next while, the two of us sat in silence with our hands resting on her letters.

That lunch was the last time I saw Deb. I can still picture how her eyes sparkled when she laughed about reading in the bathroom. I can still taste those tomatoes, summer sweet, picked that day from a neighbor's garden. But what I remember most about our lunch was the moment we realized we had been connected long before we met and how we had laughed like teenagers when we exclaimed, *"God knew!"* at the exact same time.

He was the only one who could have possibly known: That when we were little girls, we both used stories for an escape. And that when we grew up, we would use them again.

One of us told stories.

One of us read them.

I will be forever grateful to Deb for letting me tell mine.

Love, Margaret

Yes, I will remember your miracles.

—Psalm 77:11

Acknowledgments

Writing is a solitary effort, but it takes gobs of people to turn words into a book—especially this book, which began as a letter to a sick friend, the only intended reader.

I am indebted to my family and friends who gave permission to use their names here. I'm sure it feels a little weird to read about yourself in stories from the past—unless you're my dad, who will be highlighting his name on every page he's mentioned!

The following people helped me get to this moment. I am bursting with gratitude for the generous contribution they made to my work:

- Jane Resh Thomas, writing mentor extraordinaire, who taught me to look deep into my heart and write about what I found there.

- Lynne Jonell, author and friend, who read the first drafts of my coming-to-faith stories and helped me find my voice.

- Ruth Conard, missionary, minister, author, and dear friend, who held my hand and introduced me to the greatest love of my life.

- My discovery group at Woodridge Church, who taught me the power of community by loving me through my divorce and helping me find my way out of the woods each time I got lost.

- Minnesota friends Mark, Sarah, Eve, and Helayne, cheerleaders with my earliest writing—thank you for your support and for keeping me honest.

- My WOW team at Wellington Square Church: Bonnie, Fran, Heather G., Heather W., Diane, and Nancy—you guys have the biggest hearts, give the wisest counsel, and overwhelm me with all the ways you know how to love. You are WOW!

- The prayer team at Wellington Square Church, especially Heather and Penny, for praying daily blessings on Deb's letters and everyone who read them during those six months.

- Len Sweet, friend and mentor, for reaching out to a stranger with beautiful words of encouragement and for teaching me the true meaning of healing.

- Deb's sister, Darlene, for putting her own grief aside to assist me with the beginning and ending of this book.

- John and Tina, for friendship and for allowing me to retreat to Movanagher, their summer home, an Eden for writing, resting, and healing.

- Doug, for legal advice with heart and soul and for sharing the excitement of this journey.

- Jeanette Thomason, author and friend, for faith in my words and for going out on a limb to introduce me to Bryan Norman at Thomas Nelson.

- Everyone at Thomas Nelson whose talent and hard work helped make this happen. Bryan Norman, for championing this book from the start, for including me in every step of the process, and for calling me at exactly the right moments. Julie Faires and her creative team for the brilliant cover design that makes my heart go pitter-pat each time I see it. Renée Chavez, project manager, for keeping me on task, for kindly patience in teaching a newbie about the process, and for lightning response to every e-mail.

- My sister Debbie, back in my life after a lengthy absence. I love you for reading Deb's letters, for responding to them every day with encouragement and prayer, and for sharing memories of your own about growing up together.

- My baby sister, Lisa, for being my biggest fan and ally, for crying with me when I wrote about a past that was too painful to say aloud, for doing life with me shoulder to shoulder, always with hope in your heart, and for loving me through every single word I've ever written.

- My sons, Michael and Patrick, for teaching me the meaning of unconditional love and forgiveness— you have supported every decision I've made for this family even when you disagreed with my choices, you have encouraged me to keep going with my writing those days I felt I had nothing to offer, and you helped me laugh at myself when I needed it most—I am blessed beyond words to be your mom.

- And to God, for making me and for giving me a small part to play in his story.

A Few Things About Margaret . . .

I love:
- stories of random acts of kindness and how they make me smile for days.
- the change of seasons, because there's always something beginning and something ending
- the sky, for all the ways it makes me wonder about eternity
- how often I am surprised by honesty and vulnerability
- being a mom

A few years ago, I asked my dad what I was like as a little girl, and he said, "You were the happiest kid I ever knew—you were always singing and dreaming." It took me a long time to find that girl again, but I'm glad to say, she's moved back in, and I plan on keeping her around.

This is my first book, and as you read this, I'm writing away and dreaming about many more . . .

Please come visit me at margaretterry.com, on Facebook, or twitter@letters2deb.